# I Like
# Being®
# American

# I Like

# Being®

# American

*Treasured Traditions,*

*Symbols, and Stories*

Edited by

Michael Leach

D O U B L E D A Y

*New York    London    Toronto    Sydney    Auckland*

PUBLISHED BY DOUBLEDAY
a division of Random House, Inc.

DOUBLEDAY and the portrayal of an anchor with a dolphin are trademarks
of Doubleday, a division of Random House, Inc.

*I Like Being . . .*® is a trademark of Michael Leach and Therese J. Borchard. Other books in
the series include *I Like Being*® *Catholic* and *I Like Being*® *Married.*

Pages 187–190 consist of an extension of this copyright page.

*Book design by Donna Sinisgalli*

Library of Congress Cataloging-in-Publication Data

I like being American : treasured traditions, symbols, and stories /
edited by Michael Leach.— 1st ed.
p.   cm.
1. National characteristics, American—Miscellanea.   2. United
States—Civilization—Miscellanea.   I. Leach, Michael, 1940–

E169.1 .I17 2003
973—dc21            2002031250

ISBN 0-385-50743-7

PRINTED IN THE UNITED STATES OF AMERICA

February 2003
First Edition

1   3   5   7   9   10   8   6   4   2

FOR
MY FATHER

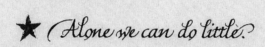

★ Alone we can do little.

Together we can do so much.
Helen Keller

# CONTENTS

Contents

# Contents

# Contents

# Contents

# I LIKE BEING AMERICAN

A Muslim cabbie in Manhattan picks up a woman rabbi at Grand Central Station. He drives her to the National Council of Churches on Riverside Drive where she has an appointment with a Catholic sister. What do these three people have in common? They like being American!

Being American does not mean living in Maine or Mississippi or Montana but having a mind-set that values life, liberty, and the pursuit of happiness wherever you are. Being an American is not so much about geographical boundaries as it is about seeing beyond limits to the spiritual qualities that make almost 300 million people *one*. It is about generosity, gratitude, peace, compassion, equality, opportunity, and freedom.

Being American is knowing that every one of us depends on all of us, and that all of us need each of us. The farmer in Cheyenne is one with the mother on welfare in Chicago. The firefighter in New Mexico is diminished when three hundred of his brethren perish in New York. And all of us are replenished when thousands of volunteers flock there to lift debris in the hope of saving a single life. Every American is Private Ryan, kneeling at the tomb of the man who saved him, and asking, "Have I lived a good life?" When Americans speak of the good life they mean far more than others elsewhere may think.

Being American is also about having flaws as large as our virtues and coming to recognize them, and, with God's grace, to regret them and make up for them. "America makes prodigious mistakes," wrote the poet e. e. cummings, "but one thing cannot be denied: America is always on the move. She may be going to hell, of course, but at least she isn't standing still."

The American dream sometimes slips into nightmare. "American history is longer, larger, more various, more beautiful, and more terrible than anything anyone has ever said about it," observed novelist James Baldwin. Our ancestors ravaged an Indian nation, chained a civilization of Africans, and killed each other in civil war. Even today we make colossal mistakes, like all nations throughout history. Yet at our best—and all countries deserve to be judged by their best—we are a people who learn from our mistakes and endeavor to extend what is best in our dream to everyone.

This book celebrates what is best about America. It shows why people with roots traceable to every corner of the earth are both proud of their heritage and grateful to be American. The American tree of life that first sprang from Europe, Africa, and Russia has grown new branches with Latin, Asian, and Middle Eastern features. It's a beautiful sight to behold, with leaves of every shape and color. And its energy comes from a single source: the desire to flourish and be free.

From vision to experience, the essays and stories in *I Like Being American* remind us of where we came from, who we are, and what we'd like to become. Most of them are original. Each one affirms a value or truth that endures. Artists, poets, and actors have always celebrated America's values on canvas, paper, and film. So this book also spotlights memorable movies, novels, and songs that inspire us to see America with fresh eyes and a warm heart. They remind us of the good that we already know but too often forget to cherish.

This is not a book then about patriotism or nationalism or any *ism*. It is simply about what the philosopher Teilhard de Chardin called "the chosen part of things." It endeavors to show, in word and picture, with pride and joy, why 300 million of us *like* being American.

—Michael Leach
July 4, 2002

# THE AMERICAN IDEA

Ours is the only country deliberately founded on a good idea.
>—John Gunther, American journalist

We hold these truths to be self-evident, that all men are created equal, that they are endowed by their Creator with certain unalienable rights, that among these are life, liberty and the pursuit of happiness. That to secure these rights, governments are instituted among men, deriving their just powers from the consent of the governed.
>—From the Declaration of
>Independence

We the people of the United States, in order to form a more perfect union, establish justice, insure domestic tranquility, provide for the common defense, promote the general welfare, and secure the blessings of liberty to ourselves and our posterity, do ordain and establish this Constitution for the United States of America.
>—From the Constitution

The people's government, made for the people, made by the people, and answerable to the people.
>—Daniel Webster, American statesman

I like being an American because America was deliberate, the intentional creation of people who wanted it more desperately than they wanted anything else. As a result, being American is a little like growing up in the house of an elegant woman who, having been loved, is herself loving.

—Phyllis Tickle
Millington, Tennessee

My eighth-grade school trip to Washington, D.C., was a defining experience. I spent a week there. I'm a patriot to the core. I love America! It was magical how the founding fathers dedicated their lives to the idea that everyone is free to live his own life.

—Ryan Bonneville
White Lake, Michigan

We are the heirs of a philosophical and political fortune. America has fostered such genius and enlightened thinking in our relatively short history that we need less to reinvent the wheels than to drive on the ones we have. We are like children of a most astounding legacy, who have forgotten where we came from. We don't need a lot of frantic action so much as we need depth of thought and historical knowledge.

—Marianne Williamson
American author
*The Healing of America*

Therefore everyone who hears these words . . . and puts them into practice is like a wise man who built his house on the rock. The rain came down, the streams rose, and the winds blew and beat against that house; yet it did not fall, because it had its foundation on the rock.

—Matthew 7:24–25

# Chapter One

# THE AMERICAN FAMILY

*E pluribus unum—out of many, one.*
                    —Motto on the Great Seal
                    of the United States

There are birds of many colors—red, blue, green, yellow—yet it is all one bird. There are horses of many colors—brown, black, yellow, white—yet it is all one horse. So cattle, so all living things—animals, flowers, trees. So men: in this land where once were only Indians are now men of every color—white, black, yellow, red—yet all one people. That this should come to pass was in the heart of the Great Mystery. It is right thus. And everywhere there shall be peace.
                    —Hiamovi (High Chief)
                    Chief of Cheyennes and Dakotas
                    *The Indian Book*

Americans are not a single ethnic group.

Americans are not of one race or one religion.

Americans emerge from all your nations.

We are defined as Americans by our beliefs—not by our ethnic origins, our race, or our religion. Our beliefs in religious freedom, political freedom, and economic freedom—that's what makes an American. Our belief in democracy, the rule of law, and respect for human life—that's how you become an American. It is these very principles—and the opportunities these principles give to so many to create a better life for themselves and their families—that make America, and New York, "a shining city on a hill."

There is no nation, and no city, in the history of the world that has seen more immigrants, in less time, than America. People continue to come here in large numbers to seek freedom, opportunity, decency, and civility.

Each of your nations—I am certain—has contributed citizens to the United States and to New York. I believe I can take every one of you someplace in New York City, where you can find someone from your country, someone from your village or town, that speaks your language and practices your religion. In each of your lands there are many who are Americans in spirit, by virtue of their commitment to our shared principles.

—Mayor Rudy Giuliani<br>
United Nations General Assembly<br>
October 1, 2001

America is not like a blanket—one piece of unbroken cloth, the same color, the same texture, the same size. America is more like a quilt—many patches, many pieces, many colors, many sizes, all woven and held together by a common thread. The white, the Hispanic, the black, the Arab, the Jew, the woman, the Native American, the small farmer, the businessperson, the environmentalist, the peace activist, the young, the old, the lesbian, the gay, and the disabled make up the American quilt.

—Jesse Jackson<br>
American human rights activist

## A Quilt of a Country
### BY ANNA QUINDLEN

America is an improbable idea, a mongrel nation built of ever-changing disparate parts, it is held together by a notion, the notion that all men are created equal, though everyone knows that most men consider themselves better than someone. "Of all the nations in the world, the United States was built in nobody's image," the historian Daniel Boorstin wrote. That's because it was built of bits and pieces that seem discordant, like the crazy quilts that have been one of its great folk-art forms, velvet and calico and checks and brocades. Out of many, one. That is the ideal.

The reality is often quite different, a great national striving consisting frequently of failure. Many of the oft-told stories of the most pluralistic nation on earth are stories not of tolerance, but of bigotry. Slavery and sweatshops, the burning of crosses and the ostracism of the other. Children learn in social-studies class and in the news of the lynching of blacks, the denial of rights to women, the murder of gay men. It is difficult to know how to convince them that this amounts to "crown thy good with brotherhood," that amid all the failures is something spectacularly successful. Perhaps they understand it at this moment [in the aftermath of 9/11], when enormous tragedy, as it so often does, demands a time of reflection on enormous blessings.

This is a nation founded on a conundrum, what Mario Cuomo has characterized as "community added to individualism." These two are our defining ideals; they are also in constant conflict. Historians today bemoan the ascendancy of a kind of prideful apartheid in America, saying that the clinging to ethnicity, in background and custom, has undermined the concept of unity. These historians must have forgotten the past, or have gilded it. The New York of my children is no more Balkanized, probably less so, than the Philadelphia of my father, in which Jewish boys would walk several blocks out of their way to avoid the Irish divide of Chester Avenue. (I was the product of a mixed marriage, across barely bridgeable lines: an Italian girl, an Irish boy. How quaint it seems now, how incendiary then.) The Brooklyn of Francie Nolan's famous tree, the Newark of which Portnoy complained, even the uninflected WASP suburbs of Cheever's characters: they are ghettoes, pure and simple. Do the Cambodians and the Mexicans in California coexist less easily today than did the Irish and Italians of Massachusetts a century ago? You know the answer.

What is the point of this splintered whole? What is the point of a nation in which Arab cabbies chauffeur Jewish passengers through the streets of New York—and in which Jewish cabbies chauffeur Arab passengers, too, and yet speak in theory of hatred, one for the other? What is the point of a nation in which one part seems to be always on the verge of fisticuffs with another, blacks and whites, gays and straights, left and right, Pole and Chinese and Puerto Rican and Slovenian? Other countries with such divisions have in fact divided into new nations with new names, but not this one, impossibly interwoven even in its hostilities.

Once these disparate parts were held together by a common enemy, by

Out of many, one? For the most pluralistic nation on earth, it's the ideal—and the reality.
AMY-BETH PITURA

the fault lines of world wars and the electrified fence of communism. With the end of the cold war there was the creeping concern that without a focus for hatred and distrust, a sense of national identity would evaporate, that the left side of the hyphen—African-American, Mexican-American, Irish-American—would overwhelm the right. And slow-growing domestic traumas like economic unrest and increasing crime seemed more likely to emphasize division than community. Today the citizens of the United States have come together once more because of armed conflict and enemy attack. Terrorism has led to devastation—and unity.

Yet even in 1994, the overwhelming majority of those surveyed by the National Opinion Research Center agreed with this statement: "The U.S. is a unique country that stands for something special in the world." One of the things that it stands for is this vexing notion that a great nation can consist entirely of refugees from other nations, that people of different, even warring religions and cultures can live, if not side by side, then on either side of the country's Chester Avenues. Faced with this diversity there is little point in trying to isolate anything remotely resembling a national character, but there are two strains of behavior that, however tenuously, abet the concept of unity.

There is the Calvinist undercurrent in the American psyche that loves the difficult, the demanding, that sees mastering the impossible, whether it be prairie or subway, as a test of character, and so glories in the struggle of this fractured coalescing. And there is a grudging fairness among the citizens of the United States that eventually leads most to admit that, no matter what the English-only advocates try to suggest, the new immigrants are not so different from our own parents or grandparents. Leonel Castillo, former director of the Immigration and Naturalization Service and himself the grandson of Mexican immigrants, once told the writer Studs Terkel proudly, "The old neighborhood Ma-Pa stores are still around. They are not Italian or Jewish or Eastern European anymore. Ma and Pa are now Korean, Vietnamese, Iraqi, Jordanian, Latin American. They live in the store. They work seven days a week. Their kids are doing well in school. They're making it. Sound familiar?"

Tolerance is the word used most often when this kind of coexistence succeeds, but tolerance is a vanilla-pudding word, standing for little more than the allowance of letting others live unremarked and unmolested. Pride seems excessive, given the American willingness to endlessly complain about them, them being whoever is new, different, unknown, or currently under suspicion. But patriotism is partly taking pride in this unlikely ability to throw all of us together in a country that across its length and breadth is as different as a dozen countries, and still be able to call it by one name. When photographs of the faces of all those who died in the World Trade Center destruction are assembled in one place, it will be possible to trace in the skin color, the shape of the eyes and the noses, the texture of the hair, a map of the world. These are the representatives of a mongrel nation that somehow, at times like this, has one spirit. Like many improbable ideas, when it actually works, it's a wonder.

**Anna Quindlen,** a Pulitzer Prize–winning columnist, is the author of the bestselling *A Short Guide to a Happy Life* and three acclaimed novels, *Object Lessons, One True Thing,* and *Black and Blue.*

Chicago is a city of neighborhoods. Mine was Polish American. It wasn't until I went to high school that I met and became friends with Irish, German, Italian, Lithuanian, and other Americans with roots in foreign lands.

I was ordained a Catholic priest in 1966 and have spent the rest of my life serving in an African American community. It's on the other side of town of my original neighborhood and yet so very close. I could not have been made to feel more welcomed anywhere on earth.

My vision of what is good and beautiful and true has simply broadened. I grew up in one community with a particular style and expression, and have moved into another with a different style and expression. I'm referring to verbal expression, food, music, ways of celebrating, spirituality, humor, and more. Each one is unique to that culture, and I have been privileged to live in and experience both.

I have learned, of course, that neither one—nor any single expression—can encompass all that is good and true and beautiful about America.

America is at once apple pie and pierogi, soul food and pasta, Tex-Mex and Cantonese. What is so wonderful about our country is precisely that: no one group has an exclusive hold on "the American idea." Catholic, Protestant, Jewish, Muslim, agnostic, or none of the above, are *all* American. Our nation was founded on this idea and I'm grateful for it. It's why I like being American, wherever I'm privileged to live and serve.

—Rev. Thomas Kaminski
Chicago, Illinois

I came to America from Middlesbrough, England, in 1973. My next intelligent choice was to marry Brigid, an Irish American girl from New York. In time we would adopt four children, two from Korea, one from Colombia, and one from Paraguay. "Only in America" is not a cliché in the Gollogly family.

I didn't become a citizen right away though. I lived in New York and enjoyed the fruits of American life but still considered myself a Brit. After our first two children, Lila and Mura, came, I took them to be naturalized at the County Courthouse in downtown Manhattan.

More than two hundred people from all over the world filled the huge courtroom, all of them eager to invest themselves in the American idea. I rubbed shoulders with people from Nigeria, Brazil,

China, Yemen, India, Haiti, and Russia. Donald Trump was even there, accompanying his wife Ivana who was born in Czechoslovakia. Brigid was home with the flu, so I had my hands full with our two new children, one and three years old. People who had come from all over the world gladly lent me a hand.

The judge came in to administer the oath, but first he spoke from his heart about the country he loved. I will never forget it.

He shared what America had meant to his grandmother who had fled pogroms in the Ukraine. She kept her naturalization certificate under her bed and would often take it out and gaze at it in gratitude. The judge stressed the profound value of a country where freedom of speech and freedom of religion were as natural as the seasons. And he talked about how we all had to work and live together, and of the privilege of paying our fair share of taxes for the things we all need in common: roads, firemen, police, ambulances, traffic lights, schools, airports, and so much more. The country could work only if everyone who lived here worked together and shared together.

Right then and there I resolved to become an American.

The judge held up ideals I could not ignore and which beat in the deepest part of my heart. "Rule Britannia," "The Queen," and all that? I loved my native England, but here in America, in the midst of diversity, I saw true democracy at work. Here was a vision that I wanted to embrace with all my heart.

I had to wait another two years for my turn to come, but when it did I could not have taken the oath more fervently, or believed in it more sincerely.

*I hereby declare, on oath, that I absolutely and entirely renounce and abjure all allegiance and fidelity to any foreign prince, potentate, state, or sovereignty of whom or which I have heretofore been a subject or citizen; that I will support and defend the Constitution and laws of the United States of America against all enemies, foreign and domestic; that I will bear true faith and allegiance to the same; that I will bear arms on behalf of the United States when required by law; that I will perform noncombatant service in the Armed Forces of the United States when required by the law; that I will perform work of national importance under civilian direction when required by the*

*law; and that I take this obligation freely without any mental reser-*
*vation or purpose of evasion; so help me God. In acknowledgment*
*whereof I have hereunto affixed my signature.*

From that day on I have been grateful to be a member of the American family.

—Gene Gollogly
New York, New York

America has been my home for sixty-three years. Gratitude fills my heart every time I gaze at the Statue of Liberty and think of the hundreds of thousands of immigrants that she has welcomed. I am filled with gratitude as I walk the halls of Congress and realize that we have a democratic form of government, that we are free of political oppression. I give thanks for the Redwoods of California, the mountains of Montana, our "old man" Mississippi, the prairies of Nebraska, the lakes of Minnesota, the rough coasts of Maine, and, being from Green Bay, the Packers. Joy fills my heart as we, nationwide, remember our military personnel on Memorial Day, sit at a table at Thanksgiving in November, illumine a July night in celebration of independence. My soul finds nourishment in reading Lincoln's Gettysburg Address, our Constitution, the Bill of Rights. I give thanks for our educational institutions: one-room schoolhouses, our prestigious universities, our pragmatic technical schools, our libraries and museums. I am grateful that we, as Americans, can say "one nation under God" and "liberty and justice for all."

—Bishop Robert Morneau
Green Bay, Wisconsin

There's something about the folks in Green Bay, Wisconsin, sitting out there in 0°F weather cheering for the Packers that makes me smile. Likewise when I've gone up to Boston and seen the lobstermen dropping their catch near the pier where some malcontents threw English tea into the harbor 227 years ago, I had to grin.

Once I stood fascinated for twenty minutes on Cannon Beach, Oregon, watching an artist paint "Haystack Rock," the towering monolith just off shore. I got the same feeling of well-being sitting on a rock in Sedona, Arizona. Walking the streets of Savannah, Georgia, is a throwback experience. The same kind of haunting atmosphere pervades New Orleans.

Woodstock, Vermont, is an almost perfect looking town. Everything is just right, especially in early October when the autumn leaves are in full glory. Carmel, California, is touristy but just about perfect as well. Jackson Hole, Wyoming, is a town you'll remember. Other places that will stay with you are Santa Fe, New Mexico; Marfa, Texas; Mackinac, Michigan; Newport, Rhode Island; Aspen, Colorado; and Loudoun County, Virginia. In all these places, folks want to tell you about the magic of their surroundings. There is a regional pride in every part of America. It is one of our strongest and most enduring qualities.

—Bill O'Reilly
American journalist, *Parade*

Lake Wobegon isn't Minneapolis. Vive la différence!

—Garrison Keillor
American storyteller

I love being an American, and my story includes an immigrant past like that of other Americans. My mother, Mary Vierra, was a Portuguese immigrant. In other ways, my story is different from most: my father, Albert Campbell, was a Northern Cheyenne Indian.

In many ways my story is the American story: I am the only American Indian serving in the United States Senate, and am one of forty-four Chiefs of the Northern Cheyenne Tribe.

America is the land of opportunity. I am proud and honored to be the first American Indian to chair the Indian Affairs Committee.

I am also a husband, father, and now a proud grandfather, and I am happy to know that my grandchildren will grow up in America—and will be able to express themselves freely because of the sacrifices of years past, to work hard and achieve a measure of material success, and to work together to build a future for themselves and their families in the most powerful and free country the world has ever seen.

—Ben Nighthorse Campbell
United States Senator (Colorado)

My forefathers didn't come over on the Mayflower, but they met the boat.

—Will Rogers, American humorist
who was of Native American descent

My name is Michael Ramirez, I am of the Kinyaa'aanii (Towering House People), and Nakai Dine' (Hispanic People). I am half Native American, a member of the Navajo tribe, and half Hispanic. I came from Mother Earth, and there is no other part of the earth that I would want to be from than America. The great diversity in America is evident; all I have to do is look at myself and I see it. Being a part of two different cultures and living in a third makes each day a new and exciting challenge: who do I want to be today or tomorrow, Navajo or Hispanic? That is a choice that I am free to make, and only in America.

—Michael Ramirez
Westbrook, Maine

People told me at the beginning, "You're too Latin for the Americans, too American for the Latins." But that's who I am. I'm Cuban American. I'm not one thing or the other. I have an American head and a Cuban heart.

—Gloria Estefan
American singer/songwriter

America was never merely a melting pot. It was, and is, a tapestry of many colors, beliefs, and cultures in which no group should ever feel it has to submerge or ignore its individuality and heritage. A robust and vibrant America requires the full contribution of many ethnic, racial, and religious groups.

—Daniel P. Moynihan
former Senator of New York

The highlight of my trip (to New York in spring 2001) came Friday night, when three of my friends and I experienced Dralion, Cirque du Soleil's avant-garde circus-arts spectacle under the big top and the events and scenery surrounding it. We took a ferry across the Hudson River to Liberty State Park. The cast of Dralion—fifty-six artists from eight countries (Brazil, Bulgaria, Canada, China, France, Ivory Coast, Ukraine, and the United States)—symbolized all that is American. Indeed, the individual artists (only a few are American citizens) looked exactly like us—an international audience. As the artists performed, the crowd of several thousand celebrated. I looked around and felt fortunate to be in a nation that embraces so many differences.

—Bill Maxwell, American columnist
*St. Petersburg Times*

Settled by the people of all nations, all nations may claim her for their own. You cannot spill a drop of American blood without spilling the blood of the whole world. . . . Our blood is as the flood of the Amazon, made up of a thousand noble currents all pouring into one. We are not a nation, so much as a world!

—Herman Melville, American novelist

Our schools, perhaps more than any other public institution, bring together children and therefore families of every race, ethnicity, and religion. Muslim girls in headscarves go to class with friends wearing elaborate, colorful braids. Parents help schools celebrate holidays of different cultures with home-cooked food representing their varied cultures, from hummus to jerk chicken to knishes to bologna sandwiches on white bread.

But none of this substitutes for learning about the great history of our nation and the freedoms that generations of Americans have fought to protect. It is important for schools to teach about democracy, about the values that include respect for human rights and individual differences and, at the same time, provide our children an understanding of what brings us together. . . . We need to find strength in our diversity and reject cynicism and bigotry in order to ensure our children's future.

—Sandra Feldman, President
American Federation of Teachers

America accepts an astounding amount of diversity from race and ethnicity to music and food to the types of cars we drive. That is so great. I'm proud of the enormous things we have accomplished as one people. And I'm proud that each of us has the opportunity to influence what America becomes.

—Janel Hanmer
Madison, Wisconsin

Printed on the loose change in our pockets is the motto from the Great Seal of the United States: *E Pluribus Unum*—"From Many, One." The words are so familiar to us, we scarcely stop to think what they mean. What is the measure of our manyness? What is the meaning of our oneness? Like any good symbol, these words are capable of stretching in many directions. Their meanings have amplified from the time the motto was first adopted in 1782. It had a political meaning then—from many colonies, one republic; from many states, one nation. . . . With the booming immigration of the late nineteenth and early twentieth centuries, the motto took on a cultural dimension—from many peoples or nationalities, one people. My own Swedish ancestors were part of the European many. How we became one is a story written out in the successive generations of our families. My mother married another Swede, but my mother's sister Irene married an Italian, Uncle Romeo, whose father had hopped on a Lake Como cruise boat in Bellano, Italy, never to return. Her sister Carolyn married Uncle Roger, whose parents were Polish. Students in my seminar tell their own versions of the story: "On my mother's side, part English and part Irish, and on my father's side, Polish and French, and perhaps some Lithuanian," they will say. These are the *E pluribus unum* stories, and America's family album is filled with them.

Today our cultural differences are magnified with the new immigration. It's not just Swedes and Italians, Lutherans and Catholics, but Russian and Iranian Jews, Pakistani and Bengali Muslims, Trinidadi and Gujarati Hindus, Punjabi Sikhs and Sindhi Jains. Creating the *unum* from the *pluribus* is now more challenging than ever.

—Diana L. Eck, American educator
*A New Religious America*

Unity in diversity is a principle that demands of us personal maturity. We must develop the ability to tolerate the creative chaos of many voices and opinions all expressing themselves at once; to not seek control over the thoughts or behaviors of others just because they are different from us; and to listen with respect and recognize the dignity of those with whom we disagree. It is not a first principle in America that any one group gets to be *right*. It is a first principle that each of us, and each of our many cultures, has valuable things to say and to contribute. Allowing everyone to do so is central to our liberty, our genius, and our evolution toward greater good.

Wrote St. Thomas Aquinas, "We must love them both, those whose opinions we share and those whose opinions we reject. For both have labored in the search for truth and both have helped us in the finding of it."

. . . Liberty depends on our understanding that America *belongs to all of us*. Equality means that none of us is inherently better than anyone else. Freedom means that we actually like it this way.

—Marianne Williamson
American author
*The Healing of America*

What would bug the Taliban more than seeing a gay woman in a suit surrounded by Jews?

—Ellen DeGeneres
hosting the 2001 Emmy Awards

Everything I Know About Being an American
I Learned in My Family
BY DONNA CRISSEY

To me, being an American is much like being a small nut on a large family tree. We're all part of the whole, but each of us carries the ability to branch in different directions and adapt to new environments.

I have a large, diverse family. My father had four brothers and a sister.

My mother had four brothers and three sisters. I am the youngest of their eight children. I have almost forty first cousins. That's a lot of nuts!

With apologies to Robert Fulghum, the lessons learned from being one of many in a family are the same fundamentals that make America great:

* No matter what your opinion is, someone disagrees with it. You have the right to feel the way you do. So do they.
* Be understanding about differences. You are different too.
* The big guys have to watch out for the little guys. It's not always fun, but it's just what you've got to do.
* You don't always have to like someone as long as you show them love and respect.
* God is God. He has many names.
* Respect each other's property and privacy. It's the old "do unto others" thing and it works.
* Share. Pain, happiness, wealth, and popcorn are all better when shared.
* Stand up for what you believe in, even if it goes against the majority.
* If you're right, they'll hear you. If you're wrong, they'll ignore you.
* If you don't know, ask! If they don't know, ask someone else. If you're not sure they're right, look it up. "Because I say so" shouldn't satisfy anyone.
* It's important to be a good neighbor. Be helpful, be friendly, share your life. Be there when you're needed but allow them the privacy you'd like in return.
* Greed ruins everything.
* Family traditions should be passed on to your children. Family prejudices should not.
* When you sit down at the table, make sure to take only your share so there's enough to go around.
* Don't ask if you can help. Just do it. Something always needs to be done and someone could always use a hand doing it.
* Watch out for squirrels.

**Donna Crissey** lives in McHenry, Illinois, with her husband, John, and her canine-kids, Buddy and Tolkien. She says she spends her time alternately destroying and rebuilding parts of their home while trying to decide what she wants to be when she grows up.

We are a multiracial, multiethnic country—a national mosaic where all the pieces come together to make a picture that is the envy of the world. Nothing could give us a greater asset for the twenty-first century than our diversity.

—Bill Clinton
Forty-second President of the
United States

Our common identity as Americans permits opposites to come together and form something higher and better than either could alone. Each person, free to be independent, is then free to be interdependent, to become part of a team that collectively reaches greater heights than any of its members could achieve alone. We are one nation—a *one* made up of *many*—under God. Is it any wonder that here the interdenominational Thanksgiving service was born?

—Alan Anderson and Deb Whitehouse
Holiday, Florida

*We, the people without a race,*
*Without a language;*
*Of all races, and of none;*
*Of all tongues, and one imposed;*
*Of all traditions and all pasts,*
*With no tradition and no past.*
*A patchwork and an altar piece.*

—Amy Lowell, American poet
"The Congressional Library"

## Freedom

BY ALEX HALEY

If Freedom were a sound, we would hear it as a titanic brass voice—clear and mighty and unaccompanied—from a wide open mouth. Together with tenors, sopranos and altos, Freedom's acoustics would swell off the voices that reverberate off the lofty ceilings of an old, medieval church.

Quite a powerful image, that Freedom. Indeed, can you imagine Freedom sounding tinny? Scratchy?

The reason I chose sound to represent my image of Freedom is because sound—or song—is intangible too, yet so rich and powerful in the way it moves those who listen and guide their lives by it. It gives the listener a reason to feel. Feelings are potent stuff, and have moved many men and women to stand up for their rights, many times, alone.

But that mighty bass voice—an individual—is what makes Freedom so mighty. Freedom is propelled by people just like you and me who desire to speak their minds. We are fortunate to live in a country that hands it to us as a birthright. No country or system is perfect, however, and over the years, those who believed that their due freedom was held back from them, spoke up. It's not magic that creates movements and marches. It's the individuals who opened their mouths.

Standing alone, speaking up, gives us strength—the backbone that makes a man or a woman. It means taking that big gulp of air and paying no heed to your sweaty palms and speaking your mind and heart, regardless of the consequences. Sometimes, we may not feel so titanic when we speak up. It may shrivel our innards and we may want to take back what took us so long to get out. Even though our voice may have sounded shaky, it's the meaning behind the words and the willingness to speak that count. In our country, Freedom is available. It's up to us to use it, and speak up when we need to. It's our right, our liberty, and, most important, our choice.

**Alex Haley**, American journalist and novelist, authored *Roots*.

# Chapter Two

# THE AMERICAN EXPERIENCE

I've always had a spirit that leaps and stretches beyond the bounds. This seed of freedom was planted and nourished in my young days on our farm in northwest Iowa. It was there, on our hundred sixty acres of land, that I lived and explored all the nooks and crannies of the grove, the creek, the pasture, the cornfields, and the extensive garden that we always had every summer. It was on this land that I tasted the spaciousness of sky and the largesse of fields while I wandered and wondered in a world that did not hem me in.

It was in that space I felt the freedom of the many wild creatures who shared our farm with us: swooping barn swallows, little wild rabbits in spring nests, the large barn owl that hooted in the night, flocks of geese in v-formation honking their way north or south, the kittens born in the barn who never did get tamed. All these creatures instilled in me a desire to be as free as they were.

Freedom came naturally. It was just there as I played outdoors and later helped with planting and harvesting the grain that grew in the farm's black, rich soil. As I breathed in the fresh air on dewy mornings and savored the fragrance of newly mown alfalfa fields I was oblivious to the harsh reality of the many people in other parts of the world who experienced enforced confinement and fear. Only years later did I come to realize what an immense treasure I had as a child. To this day I still appreciate and long for unconfined space where I can move without the fetters of physical space and the constraining ideologies that bind my body and mind. Always I will be grateful for the gift of growing up on a farm that gave my spirit wings and room to roam.

—Joyce Rupp
Dubuque, Iowa

I'm a young Asian American who lives in Brooklyn, works in midtown Manhattan near Times Square, and hangs out in the heart of the City when the sun goes down.

At times after work, I love to walk down Broadway to the East Village or Chinatown just to see what new stores are opening or take in the liveliness around me in "the city that never sleeps." When I'm walking downtown I can smell the fresh roasted peanuts and pretzels that vendors sell on street corners or listen to poets hawking their beliefs or be amazed by the photos of the city that photographers sell from makeshift stands. Sometimes I stop and take a look at the ordinary things I miss sitting in an office all day while the sun is outside and tourists are exploring this magical city.

But the most fun I have is going to Chinatown.

Every so often my friends and I go there for Dim Sum that you can smell from a block away. We wander around Canal Street purchasing T-shirts, slippers, CDs, movies, earrings, eyeglasses, shoes, and Chinese candies that you can't find anywhere else. We eat a delicious but inexpensive dinner in Chinatown and then get cappuccino and desserts in Little Italy which is just a hop, skip, and a jump away.

These little things hint at why I love being an American and a New Yorker. I can be anything I want here, and experience other cultures that run through American culture like roots in a great tree. That's what's great about this country: you can cross the street in a big city and experience someone else's culture and know it is also somehow your own. Everything can be found here—both old and new—and anything is possible.

—Vanessa Wong
Brooklyn, New York

New York, New York . . . a city made up of foreign countries you can visit for the price of a subway token.

—Zev Chafets, American columnist
*New York Daily News*

For thirty years my work has taken me across America's terrain. I found healing from grief and loss on the Eastern seacoast where I was raised. I explored the Western desert, questing for vision in landscapes of rock and cactus. Ultimately, I made the hills of the Southwest my home. Knowing that my heart will always travel through changing frontiers, I love it that America offers rich and varied lands to match the moving geography of my soul.

—Paula D'Arcy
Kerriville, Texas

Jerry and I do not own a traditional home, or even an address. Our residence is a 30-foot motor home we call Homer. We tow Jethro, our trusty "toad," for adventures in smaller locales. The treasures from our pre-retirement life are in storage for our next lifestyle, maybe ten years down the road. Right now we're appreciating life as nomads in this vast and beautiful land, and we don't want to stop.

We've visited twenty-four states, from Washington to Georgia, in four years. Family celebrations and illnesses dictate a lot of our schedule but oh, what journeys we've been on! We've traveled warm and dry through four hurricanes, skirted a tornado in Ohio, and found our way out of a lunar labyrinth in North Dakota's Badlands (did you know that Theodore Roosevelt has a National Park there?). We've driven alongside antelope, coyote, and bison as well as cars, trucks, and moving vans. We carry what we need wherever we go.

After 9/11 Jerry felt proud and I was comforted to see flags waving from almost every home, business, and school. Banners draped over bridges and overpasses expressed love and support for our fellow Americans in New York, Washington, and Pennsylvania. Jerry and I don't have a traditional address but we are at home in America wherever we happen to be.

—Mary Anne Stevens
On the road

As a manager for a global company I take frequent trips abroad. For some reason I always seem to miss something interesting while on the road. I was in Mexico City when McGuire broke the home run record, Lisbon when the Lewinsky scandal broke, and Madrid when the Florida recount was tallied. Being outside of the United States for events like these brings a unique sense of fun. Foreign people don't get it, and it's not hard to see why. Yet their collective sense of bewilderment makes me feel connected to a spirit larger than myself. I understand what's happening back home and in some strange way it always makes me feel good about being American.

—Jeff Leach
Washington, D.C.

I have always been proud to be an American but never thought about it in those words until now. In my family, being proud meant being proud to be a Virginian. This heritage began with the first settlers of Virginia, and as a child my first years in school seemed to be centered on learning about Virginia and its famous people and contributions to the growth of the United States. And always in the background was the sense of responsibility that we felt to maintain our country the way our forefathers had envisioned. We moved to New York when I was ten, and I quickly learned that not only my southern drawl but my focus on Virginia and ancestors was only a source of ridicule. I adapted quickly and soon lost my accent and learned the value of accepting a wide view of this country. Not just one state in 48, but being one of 48, and later 50, equal partners. World War Two cemented these ideals, and a deep love of country grew even though it waxed and waned over the next fifty years. Now in my eighties, as I see my children and grandchildren finish their education, take advantage of job opportunities, become part of a community, I offer my deepest and most reverent prayers, thankful that they are lucky enough to live in a country where they can choose where to live, how to earn a living, what to believe, and to experience sharing and belonging without dictates controlling their every move. I still have a deep pride in my Virginia heritage, but all that really means is that I am a part of the beginning of America and proud and happy to be able to say those words—"I am an American."

—Julie Firman
Amherst, Massachusetts

Growing up on Barry Avenue in Chicago's Lakeview neighborhood in the 1950s, my world was decidedly small. But whose wasn't back then, especially when they were only six years old?

One set of grandparents lived upstairs; the other was about six blocks away. Most aunts, uncles, and cousins were within walking distance, which was a good thing, since my family didn't own a car.

The major landmarks in my life were St. Alphonsus Church—big, beautiful, and gothic with exquisite stained glass from Munich—and St. Alphonsus School—fourteen hundred well-behaved students in classes of fifty or more—both less than two blocks from my front door.

When I was six I knew I was an American, I knew I was a Catholic, but I also heard older relatives talking about being German in a place called "The Old Country." My grandmothers would talk German to each other and to their friends, especially when they did not want us kids to know what they were saying. I knew that when my mother sent me to the store around the corner on Lincoln Avenue there was a pretty good chance I'd have to point to what I wanted because the clerk only spoke German. One week a whole bunch of new kids arrived at school. They spoke German and wore the same clothes as the people pictured on Grandpa's fancy beer steins. They were lucky that old Sister Donata could speak their language.

German people came to St. Alphonsus from all over the Chicago area to be married by a priest who spoke their language. I was often assigned to be the altar boy. After hearing them dozens of times, I memorized the marriage vows in German. Unfortunately that was all the German I learned despite several years of Saturday morning German-language classes under Sister Radegunde's tutelage.

As a youngster growing up, I thought the whole world was like my neighborhood. Turns out that I was living in one of the largest German enclaves outside Europe! America is like that. Lucky me! It's great to be an American.

Oh, yes—those new German-speaking students were refugees of the 1956 Hungarian uprising. I still see some of them on occasional forays into the old neighborhood, and they, too, are glad to be Americans!

—Thomas R. Artz
Chicago, Illinois


I wasn't always an American. The wind in my hair in my youth came across the fields from Connemara or Sligo after already crossing the Atlantic from America. My mother, who had been there, told us children about Seattle and New York and going to see Charlie Chaplin in *The Gold Rush*. Seeds were sown in the imagination. Hope was planted in the poor fields: not as big a hope as heaven but the best interim dream we knew.

I sailed into New York Harbor on the good ship *Brittania*. The train from Grand Central Station to Chicago stopped unaccountably in the countryside outside Buffalo. I looked through the window into the darkness and saw America and loved what I saw— potential as big as all existence.

Later, John F. Kennedy came and went. Americans walked on the moon. The Vietnam War dropped Agent Orange on my psyche. Shocking that such a poor country so far away could leave such scabs on such a great place as America. Then there was Nixon and Marilyn Monroe and Mickey Mantle and Broadway and the Ford Edsel and Dear Abby and Ed McMahon diligently laughing at Johnny Carson's jokes late at night.

I became a U.S. citizen, one of several hundred that day, from nearly every creed and country, getting a new baptism amid unquenchable hope in America's potential to renew itself and then inspire the world to do the same. We were each given a festive balloon. I tied mine to a spider plant in my study and it banged its head against the ceiling with elation.

I have in the meantime visited three of America's four corners, symbolically speaking. I met famous people but mostly I met people. The darkness I saw from the train lifted and I saw that America in real life is not only an ideal but also a country where some get shot and others get filthy rich and sometimes the filthy rich get shot as well in the land of equal opportunity. There have been triumphs and disasters, some of which came to my door, but the big ones passed by. The Twin Towers came and went. The balloon that was so buoyant one April years ago is now shriveled, but it still clings to the same plant, which refuses to die.

America is not only a country but an ideal. It has never stopped holding aloft the Great Gatsby hope that all the potential will become reality some sunny day.

The same wind still blows my hair gone gray. Now it comes across the plains of Kansas after already crossing the Pacific from God knows where. It's an indefatigable wind that never gives up.

—Michael Farrell
Kansas City, Kansas


I grew up hearing my father say, over and over, like a mantra, "Antoinette, this is the best country in the world. Don't ever forget it."

Dad always got a faraway look in his eyes when he said that, and sometimes I could note a trace of a tear. When I was older I learned more of his life, how he left his Calabria in Italy at age thirteen in the midst of World War I. He began a three-year trek, life-threatening from hunger and war battles, that took him through Italy and France, before he was able to get on a boat to America.

Toni Bosco with her dad in 1946: "I learned great lessons."

In this new country he experienced what he had dreamed of, a life where people had freedom, giving them the right to earn a living, have a family, get an education, vote for officials, worship God, and help others.

Always remembering his starving days in Europe, my father,

who became owner of a meat and vegetable market, carried out his own private mission of never turning away the hungry. As a youngster, I worked with him, saw how subtly he handed bags of food to purse-poor people, and I learned great lessons. All he did was possible, my father would say, because he had come to "the best country in the world."

My father was not oblivious to flaws and problems here, but he loved being an American, and I who saw my homeland through his eyes and heart, from an early age on knew it was a privilege to be an American.

—Antoinette Bosco
Brookfield, Connecticut

My father would make out returns until three or four in the morning, and I'd ask him, "Don't you hate doing this?" He would give me this long lecture. "It's a great privilege to pay your taxes, and you should overpay your taxes"—which I do actually—"and just think of all those people who would like to come to America just to have the privilege to pay taxes. Better pay every single penny of them. And better make sure you don't take anything that doesn't belong to you." As I got older, I started to realize what it was about. It was extremely conscious, well thought out. And very overdone.

—Rudy Giuliani, former Mayor of
New York, *Time* magazine

*Eleftheria* is the Greek word for "freedom," and this is a word that both my parents often expressed during my developmental years. "You can become anything you want to be if you work hard. This is a great country and you are free to make choices." I never forgot those words, and I cherish the fact that I am an American. Both my parents were Greeks who were born in Izmir, survived the persecution of the Turks, and fled for their lives to America. Both college graduates, they instilled in me the desire to excel in school, college, and graduate school; to choose carefully; and to always honor all the American holidays and traditions. Their favorite holiday was Thanksgiving, and despite the fact that my mother was an accomplished Greek cook, she made everything "American," including cranberry sauce and pumpkin pie, neither of which is found in Greek cuisine. To this day, I, too, love Thanksgiving . . . the parade, the food, even the football games.

Although I was raised in a very Greek home, not allowed to date anyone who wasn't Greek, and had a predominately Greek circle of friends, I was encouraged to participate in any activities that aroused my curiosity. Cooking became one of my hobbies. When I was a junior winner in the Pillsbury Baking contest, I was thrilled to win with something very typical, very American: a pound cake!

My Greek heritage is still very much a part of my life today, but I have tried to instill my love of being an American in my children. Over the years, I got involved in the PTA, serving as president at several levels, the Boy Scouts, serving as a den mother, and working with the Girl Scouts, handling endless cookie sales. With the tragedy of September 11, I am proud to reaffirm my love of my country by donating time and money for those in need. I believe that everything I do goes back to that word *eleftheria,* freedom, and being free to make choices. I guess that's why I love being an American.

—Katherine R. Boulukos
Freeport, New York


Others might describe my family heritage as Cherokee, Welsh, and English, but I grew up describing myself as an American to any person who might have asked. Few asked in those days.

I grew up in Seattle during the time of the Hungarian revolution and unrest in Russia and Northern Europe. Just like today, world problems brought many of my friends' families to America. But we all formed deep, unbreakable friendships because we shared so many totally American experiences, usually at school or church. For example, my dearest best friend, Tove Pors, was born in Norway. We met for the first time when we signed up for the church choir and youth group. We still keep in touch, talking about our children and occasionally a shared experience from childhood. The most common ideal my friends and I experienced was the unity in diversity that is the heart of being American. Many of my friends had new Anglicized surnames like Beck, Mills, Angel, or Waters, but their parents spoke English with accents that echoed faraway lands. Most of the people I knew were from "somewhere else originally." This common acceptance of diversity helped eliminate prejudices that could have damaged the fragile fibers of teenage friendships. Differences were the norm so it was a nonissue to most of us.

Today my childhood experiences are being repeated in many different parts of America. Children from Asia, Latin America, Africa, and the Middle East are also sharing the same American experiences, with each other and with the grandchildren of the Becks, Mills, Angels, and Waters. To grow up with a wealth of friendships, sharing diversity, is one of the best aspects of our American heritage.

Growing up in Seattle made it easy for me to marry someone from another country. My own wonderful husband, an Arab Christian from Syria, I met in New York. Watching his experiences as an immigrant, I learned to appreciate how difficult it is to reestablish one's self in a new land. But hard as it was for him, he deeply loves and cherishes the vast opportunities—and the unity amidst diversity—that America offers him and our three sons.

—Wanda Munfakh
Manhasset, New York

Yes, we are proud of the groups to which we belong but it's what comes after the hyphen of Czech-American, African-American, Asian-American, or any other variety of American, that counts most. No matter our race or creed, we are all equal shareholders in the American dream.

—Madeleine Albright
former Secretary of State

## Haven for Humanity
### BY CAROL MOSELEY-BRAUN

I am a black woman. I have on occasion asked God why this condition of my birth has been such a defining aspect of my being. The gift of life, it seems to me, should be enough for all of us to be allowed to make our own unique contribution to humanity. Recognizing, however, that that is a hopelessly naïve view of existence, I have had to come to grips with the stark reality that the skin I am in makes me the least powerful, the least respected, the least valued of all of God's children on this earth.

That is why I am really glad to have been born in America.

This country was formed out of an idealistic vision that made individual happiness the foundations of its fundamental political compact. Individual freedom has always been a core value for Americans, and this respect for the essential humanity of each person has rarely been embraced as an aspect of national identity as it has here. By defining the political compact as arising out of the consent and support of each person, American democracy underscores a belief in the Godliness of humanity.

The history of our country makes it all too plain that we did not live up to the idealism of that vision even while we debated and adopted our Declaration of Independence. Not only slavery, but the disenfranchisement of women, the genocide of Native Americans, the exploitation of the poor—all these and more can and have been held up as proof of the hypocrisy of our founding charters. Dr. Martin Luther King once referred to the Declaration of Independence as a Declaration of Intent. I think that he precisely described the aspect of our political compact that for me, in my time, is so compelling. The intent, the vision, the objective of America is grounded in an ecumenical commitment to make our country a haven for humanity like no other on this planet. My country has from the beginning held out the moral vision toward which it has over time aspired. The Declaration of Intent is a reflection of a universally held belief among Americans, and one to which reference has been made time and again as we have grappled with perfecting our democracy and living up to that ideal.

> *We hold these truths to be self-evident, that all men are created equal, that they are endowed by their Creator with certain unalienable rights, that among these are life, liberty and the pursuit of happiness.*

These words inspire Americans, because they speak to the highest and most noble ideals of our national identity.

I was born on the very day that Jackie Robinson signed with the Brooklyn

Carol Moseley-Braun, the first African American woman to be elected a United States Senator and later an ambassador, receives a service award from New Zealand Prime Minister Helen Clark at the home of Sir Robert Jones.

Dodgers baseball team. This was for me personally a signal achievement, because it marked the beginning of the end of American apartheid. My most vivid memory of segregation is of my little brother being confused by a water fountain sign that said: COLORED WATER. He thought it meant water that was green and red and blue and yellow. He did not understand the explicit limitation referred to *his* color. We were spared the worst part of segregation, and I grew up in a hopeful time when white America reminded itself of the Declaration of Intent and began to rid itself of the contradictions of race-defined citizenship. The strides made by black Americans to become fully integrated in their country's society during my lifetime have been unparalleled. I cannot imagine what it must have been like to have been born in a time when my color would have limited my citizenship or even my very movements in America.

I was born at a time when women, too, began to enjoy the blessings of liberty. We are today appalled that the Taliban regime in Afghanistan refused even the basic civil rights to women, but forget that even American women were similarly situated within the last century. American women can vote, can work, can contribute in every aspect of our society now; but it has not always been so. I am the beneficiary of the women who demanded the rights our basic political compact promised every person, and I am the product of their insistence on equality. As America reminded itself of its promise, and recognized in sexism a useless waste of human talent, women began to enjoy choices about their lives in ways that serve the whole community. I cannot imagine a time when my gender would have limited my citizenship or my right to earn a living in America.

This hopeful, optimistic, progressive time has moved America closer to its Declaration of Independence than any other time in her history. It has given people like me the confidence that someday *all* of the barriers to human accomplishment and contribution will be removed, and neither wealth nor physical ability nor geography will limit the range of individual achievement. In all my travels around the world, I have nowhere felt the sense of possibility that these times give Americans. For all the travails and struggles, arguments and debates, we are joined in a belief in the correctness of our vision and the inevitable triumph of liberty and justice for all.

That is why I am glad to be an American, and why I hope in my public service to help share the blessings of this vision with the world.

**Carol Moseley-Braun** teaches at Morris Brown College and is an attorney with Goodworks International in Atlanta, Georgia. She is former U.S. Ambassador to New Zealand and Samoa, and former United States Senator from Illinois (the first African-American woman in history to be elected to the Senate).

I once heard Oprah Winfrey say, "If you're a woman born in America, you're one of the luckiest women in the world." How true that is. My parents, even though poor, saved all they had and gave my three sisters, my brother, and me a college education. After graduation I chose to move from a small town in Mississippi to New York and got my first job as a claims rep for the Social Security Administration. I married my "prince" when I was twenty-three, and even though it was tough at the beginning to make ends meet, I was able to stay at home and raise our two sons until they were in elementary school. I first volunteered and then got a job as a teacher's aide in their school and became so interested in helping children with learning disabilities that I took night courses at a university for four years and got a master's degree in education. I chose to go back to work full-time at age forty as a learning disabilities teacher. I'm now assistant principal of an inner-city school. What a blessing to have so many choices, at every stage of life! Oprah is right: "If you're a woman born in America, you're one of the luckiest women in the world."

—Vickie Leach
Riverside, Connecticut

33

## No Walls

BY SETAREH SABETY

All year long I live a pretty isolated life in this rural corner of Maryland. I remember when I first came here from Iran, the vast open spaces made me feel agoraphobic. Lack of friends or a social life made me feel extremely lonely. I longed for the tall walls and the long conversations of my childhood.

But now, after a couple of years of this loneliness, I have come to love it. At first I took the neighbors' distancing of themselves as coldness. But now I realize that it comes from a profound respect for the other's independence that is peculiarly American. No one engages in superficial pleasantries in our town, but if your car breaks down they stop immediately and help.

Here in America you can live a whole life on a street and not know the person who lives across from you. This can be seen as a lack of caring or warmth, but if you give it a chance you will see that it is indeed a blessing. It comes from nothing more or less than a respect for other people to be "other," to have their home and live in it as they wish. How many compatriots would exchange the womblike comfort of the Persian home for this kind of prairie freedom?

In our parts of the world, the wall is a great, almost too obvious, metaphor for how we live, how we see, and how we are seen. Nothing is said or expressed directly. All discourse has to circumvent the wall or leak through it. It is hard to keep a conversation open and civil when shouting it over a wall or whispering it through a crack.

It is a comforting architectural fixture, the wall. It keeps the heat in and the bad people out. The wall protects from the elements, but it is confining. In order to see beyond it one must necessarily climb or demolish it. In order to climb or bring down a wall one must have determination and strength and resilience.

But here in this youthful greenness that surrounds this particular corner of the American landscape, there are no walls cutting through one's line of vision. Here you can see forever. This foreverness of the landscape allows one to think and dream and never be encumbered with who thinks what about what one wears. Here in this limitless, open-ended vastness that seems to go to the end of the world, the neighbors, by their blessed lack of interest, allow you to be who you want to be. Here no one judges you because they simply do not care; they are too busy trying to live their own dreams.

The family who lives across from me may be fascists, for all I know, but their respect for my independence, and the law that guarantees it, will always keep them civil. More civil than many a like-minded Iranian. More civil than people who pretend to be friends but engage in the most cutting gossip the minute you have left their company.

Here we are all linked by one thing alone and that is our mutual respect (at least at a very basic level) for the law. That link is the most precious bond that exists between the people of this country. In America you can wear what you want, play the *donbak* all night, think and dress and drink in any way you like, as long as you pay the bills and stop at the stop sign—as long as you obey the law.

For this I am grateful to be living here. They let me be who I want to be. Here I can be Iranian and a Democrat and a mother without anyone ever questioning my motives or wondering how this *seyedeh* from Mashad ended up in Maryland. Here it is taken for granted that the person you choose to be is your choice and not the upshot of some incredibly twisted conspiracy.

The other day at the local Safeway I was talking to an elderly couple who were, like me, waiting for their ride. Although they were vocal pro-life evangelists and on the opposite spectrum of politics from me, I told them that the reason I am here and not in Iran is because I believe in the separation of church and state which this nation has championed throughout its history.

I knew that being die-hard evangelists they would not necessarily agree. But they both smiled, nodded, and understood in almost an intuitive way. Even though they were consumed by their open passion for their religion, they agreed with me on this most important of democratic principles. They did not care if I was a feminist or on the left of them ideologically; they respected my appreciation of this simple and valuable notion of keeping religion out of politics. On this subject at least there were no walls between us.

In this nation of new identities, they leave you alone to forge yours. Nowhere else gives you this opportunity in quite the same way. America provides you with as large a canvas and as varied a color palette as possible to paint your own portrait. Here freedom is about the opportunity to start anew—to be who you want to be regardless of your parentage and cultural baggage, regardless of your past. Most important, in this country they allow you to be "other" to them. For all of that I am grateful.

Here, agreeing to disagree is in people's blood—they do it automatically without a thought. Here, walls are not necessary because we need not hide our differences; we celebrate them.

I have often written about my longing for Iran. My life in exile has been one dedicated to remembering everything with the desperateness of one who knows she may never go back. But this longing and homesickness has always been thankfully accompanied by a deep and ever-growing appreciation of my adopted country, my sweet and tolerant and incredibly open-armed host: America.

**Setareh Sabety** was born in Tehran, Iran, and is a freelance writer and Internet columnist (iranian.com) living in Middletown, Maryland, with her husband and two children.

I'd much rather be a minority in this country than anyplace else in the world.

—Condoleezza Rice
National Security Affairs Advisor

## Nikki-Rosa

BY NIKKI GIOVANNI

*childhood remembrances are always a drag*
*if you're Black*
*you always remember things like living in Woodlawn*
*with no inside toilet*
*and if you become famous or something*
*they never talk about how happy you were to have*
*your mother*
*all to yourself and*
*how good the water felt when you got your bath*
*from one of those*
*big tubs that folk in chicago barbecue in*
*and somehow when you talk about home*
*it never gets across how much you*
*understood their feelings*
*as the whole family attended meetings about Hollydale*
*and even though you remember*
*your biographers never understand*
*your father's pain as he sells his stock*
*and another dream goes*
*and though you're poor it isn't poverty that*
*concerns you*
*and though they fought a lot*
*it isn't your father's drinking that makes any difference*
*but only that everybody is together and you*
*and your sister have happy birthdays and very good*

*Christmases*
*and I really hope no white person ever has cause*
*to write about me*
*because they'll never understand*
*Black love is Black wealth and they'll*
*probably talk about my hard childhood*
*and never understand that*
*all the while I was quite happy.*

**Nikki Giovanni** is an American poet.

# Chapter Three

# THE NEW AMERICAN PIONEERS

## The Typical American Family

BY RICHARD REEVES

The typical American family—you know, Mom and Dad, a couple of kids—now speaks with an accent, according to the latest census data.

Crunching new Census Bureau statistics from the year 2000, the *Washington Post* came up with this: In areas with high Hispanic and Asian populations, 25 percent of residents live in traditional married-with-children homes, compared with only 23 percent in places where there is low immigrant population. (In 1990, those numbers were almost exactly reversed, with areas with high immigrant population having fewer traditional families than the rest of the country.)

But take comfort, red-blooded Americans: As these Americans become assimilated, they will become more like us. Their family ties will unravel, too—just like ours. According to Jeffrey Passel of the Urban Institute: "The incomes go up, the education goes up, the divorce rate goes up, out-of-wedlock childbirth goes up as immigrants assimilate." In fact, we need these people desperately. Who, after all, is going to do the work? Who is going to pay my Social Security and Medicare? The lifestyles of people who change jobs (or are forced to change jobs) every three or four years, of people too busy or self-indulgent to have children, of people living healthily into their eighties (collecting benefits all the while) may or may not be fun or inspiring, but that doesn't clean the streets or pay the bills. The land of the free and the home of the old doesn't have much of a ring to it.

The effects of these demographic changes will fuel the socioeconomic, sociopolitical debate of the early twenty-first century. Learned folk will call our country a "New America."

But it is not really new. What is being called immigration is the same old wonderful American same-old. The "new" Americans are us a century and more later. Testimony from a taxi driver in Manhattan, where the last native-born driver was spotted in September of 1994: "I love America. I am starting a new generation here."

So he is. The man is from India and has a degree in physics from the University of Calcutta. His wife, who has just been credentialed as a substitute teacher in Queens, has a graduate degree in English literature from the same university. They have two children. One has just been admitted (by test) to Stuyvesant High School, the city's best public school, where an Irish immigrant named Frank McCourt taught English for more than twenty-five years. The other is in the top 5 percent of her class at a magnet school in Queens. The father is an American citizen now, but he regularly returns to India to pay real respect to his parents—because they are his parents.

He could be compared to an Italian immigrant one hundred years ago, but he and his wife had much more education and spoke the Queen's (Victorian) English long before they came to America. The people they are most like are the Americans and immigrants on the Oregon Trail in the 1840s and 1850s.

This man and his wife are not immigrants anymore. They are pioneers. Their trail happened to begin in Bengal rather than Missouri, but they are quite like the "immigrants" who went west 150 or so years ago. Those earlier pioneers traveled as families; they had to, because a man alone cannot farm effectively. And they had some money from selling the farm or a shop—or they borrowed—because it cost about $1,500 to outfit a wagon for the five-month journey over the plains and the mountains. The most successful of today's Hispanic and Asian pioneers work as families, too, because they have old-fashioned families and the American way of life isn't cheap.

Obviously most new immigrants do not have graduate degrees, but they do have family values, and their goal, like that of the Irish in the late nineteenth century, is to bring as many family members as they can to the "New World." But there were poor people on the trail, too, in the old days. The

Mormons, heading for Utah and California, made it only by pooling re-sources—and by some sharp trading.

The names and the faces change over time. But America is still America, still the new frontier for new pioneers with enough guts and willpower to get here.

**Richard Reeves** is an award-winning writer, syndicated columnist, and doc-umentary filmmaker. His many books include biographies of Presidents Kennedy and Nixon.

## *Hispanidad:* A Rainbow of Feelings, a Paradise of Sounds, a Parade of Flavors
### BY DAVID AQUIJE

I arrived in the United States in 1991 after graduating from the Inca Gar-cilaso de la Vega University in Lima, Perú, as a journalist. I did not want to leave my country behind but felt compelled to do so in order to pursue my career and my dream. Perú was going through an economic and social crisis. President Alan García Pérez had disappointed the people, appropriating the banking system for the government and opening the way to the most corrupt government in Peruvian history: that of García's successor, President Alberto Fujimori and Fujimori's chief advisor, Vladimiro Montesinos, a drug and weapons dealer. Two terrorist groups, the Shining Path and the Túpac Amaru Revolutionary Movement, were increasing their attacks in the capital. In five years, García Pérez brought Perú to 2,000 percent inflation, and in ten years the terrorists had killed twenty-five thousand Peruvians.

So I left. I was the last of nine siblings to come to the United States, com-pleting a family exodus of nearly twenty-five years. In that amazing year, 1991, we all gathered together as a family for the first time in one country at the same time. We had an unforgettable Mother's Day celebration.

My story is not different from that of 35 million other Hispanics who live here. We all came for a reason and with a dream, the simple dream of living peaceful lives with dignity. Many of us—Cubans, Guatemalans, Salvadorans,

Dominicans—have come seeking refuge from oppressive governments, civil wars or revolutions. Others, like Colombians, abandoned their country because they were afraid of being kidnapped or killed under a system rampant with corruption and drug trafficking. Mexicans have not arrived because they have always been here: they didn't cross a *frontera*; the *frontera* crossed them. That is how we Hispanics happen to be in the United States.

We are not all the same—we have different stories and skin tones. Census 2000 identified us as an ethnic group that encompasses people of any race. There are white Hispanics, black Hispanics, Hispanic Indians, Asian Hispanics, mulattos, and mestizos. We have different beliefs as well: we are Catholics, Buddhists, Jews, Santeros, Mayas, Quechuas, or Navajos. And even though we may speak different languages, we predominantly speak Spanish. The language that the *conquistadores* imposed on us became our language. We enriched it with our own words and accents, which is why a Dominican speaks differently from a Puerto Rican from a Peruvian from an Argentinean. Still, we understand each other and celebrate the meaning each one gives to a particular word. That is our culture: a rainbow of feelings, a paradise of sounds, a parade of flavors. We are woven in a beautiful tapestry we call *Hispanidad.*

Many of us Hispanic immigrants are here formally. That is, we have a work permit, a green card, or we are already naturalized citizens. Others are not. At best, they are called undocumented, at worst "illegal aliens." But all of us contribute nearly $280 billion yearly to this nation, making the United States the fifth largest Hispanic market in the world after Spain, Argentina, Mexico, and Colombia. In a few years we will be an even stronger economic presence, as it is projected that we will make this country the second largest Hispanic market. We will reach that milestone

The Aquijes, a typical American family

with our hard work. We pick tomatoes, work in supermarkets, as landscapers, and in construction; we are cooks, waiters, and busboys, nannies and house-keepers. We are writers, journalists, teachers, entertainers, comedians, musicians, and dancers. The product of our work is not illegal and it has helped boost the U.S. economy. We have filled old and desolate towns and cities with bodegas, restaurants, and other small businesses.

We are here to stay and we are proud to be Americans because we have come to build our dream with our work and sacrifice. To everything we do we add *lo nuestro*—that is, our passion, our songs, our foods, our youth. We especially bring our strong and wide sense of family. We *are* family, we teach family, we celebrate family. As Hispanics we are different yet one. That is precisely one of our greatest contributions to America: we exemplify unity in diversity.

We have not always been welcome here even though our contributions can be traced in any decade of this nation's history, a nation we have fought for in all its wars. As a modest example, when I went to the United States Consulate in Lima to receive my visa, I was asked if I would be willing to fight for this nation. It was the day before the start of the Persian Gulf War. I had not yet arrived in this country but already I had declared my willingness to defend its ideals of freedom and justice for all.

When I arrived in New York I realized no one would recognize me as a Peruvian but rather as a Hispanic. Unfortunately, as a Hispanic who could not speak English fluently, I often felt invisible, like a person who did not exist. Once I was waiting for information at a library desk, but the librarian, as if I was not there, spoke to the white lady that was coming after me. In our Latin American countries foreigners who are struggling to communicate in Spanish are treated with kindness and offered assistance. The prejudices and discrimination I felt here are some of the flaws of this system that we Hispanic Americans are fighting, with others, to banish. From them we are learning our rights and how to defend them. I feel extremely proud of being Hispanic. I am an American citizen now and in my heart I am a U.S. citizen on behalf of all my undocumented brothers and sisters.

Now I am bilingual. I communicate in English, but when I am at home I speak to my children (who are also bilingual) in Spanish. It's just that there are words such as *amigo, fiesta,* and *compadre* that have special meaning when spoken in Spanish. I also pray in *Español* because it is in this language that I first met God. And quite honestly, I am not sure that God will deliver me from evil unless I tell him: . . . *y líbrame de todo mal.*

I like being an American and I have always felt American. We Hispanics think of America not as the country with fifty states but as a single united continent. America is one continent, not three: north, central, and south. A Peruvian in New York is American just as an Italian in Rome is European; a Colombian in Chicago is American just as a Kenyan in Nairobi is African. That sense of a single America is in our blood, our history. The idea was born two centuries ago with the *Gran Libertador*, Simón Bolívar, who envisioned a great American nation from Alaska to Tierra del Fuego. While Bolívar had this dream in the south, George Washington had a similar dream in the north.

Native Americans were the first to dream in this way. An indigenous legend points out that every five hundred years the eagle and the condor are to fly in harmony. Somehow that is happening. All Hispanics who live and work here contribute to the economic bounty of our country. This includes "undocumented" workers who pay taxes yet receive no health, social security, and retirement benefits. Those who truly benefit are the companies that hire these workers and don't declare them. They have a double benefit: they do not pay taxes; they do not pay benefits as medical insurance, sick days or holidays. At the same time we contribute to the economies of our former countries because we wire money back to our families. Economies like those of Mexico and El Salvador have documented the contribution of their citizens living in foreign countries, particularly the United States. President Bush's administration has also discovered how important it is for north and south to fly in harmony. Even before September 11 changed the course of history, free trade initiatives with Latin America, the establishment of more solid democracies, and international accords to fight drug trafficking were priorities for the Bush administration. Secretary of State Colin Powell was at the General Assembly of the Organization of American States, which was being hosted by Peruvian president Alejandro Toledo in Lima, when the terrorist attacks occurred.

This is why I like being an American. I do not have to lose my Peruvian identity. To the contrary, when I received my citizenship in 1996, President Bill Clinton sent a welcoming message to the twenty-five hundred new American citizens who swore fidelity to the U.S. flag at the Jacob Javits Center in New York. He asked us not to forget our roots and to add the good things we have from our cultures because that was what being American was about.

For that reason now I am proud to say: I am David Aquije, a Limeño, a Peruvian, a descendant of the great Inca empire, a citizen of the United States, a Hispanic, Latino, mestizo, cholo, a fan of Alianza Lima, the New York Yankees, and the Metro Stars. I am proud to be a Catholic and a Democrat as I am proud to be a son and a brother, a husband and a father, a nephew, a cousin and an uncle; a coworker, a friend and a neighbor, a *compadre* and a godfather.

For all of these humble blessings I *love* being an American.

**David Aquije** is associate editor of *Revista Maryknoll.* He and his wife, Rosa, live in Wappingers Falls, New York, with their three children, Fiorella Isabel, David Gabriel, and Abbey Carolina (how's that for a "paradise of sounds"!).

Latinos have come to the United States to seek the same dreams that have inspired millions of others: they want a better life for their children. Family values do not stop at the Rio Grande River. Latinos enrich our country with faith in God, a strong ethic of work and community and responsibility. Immigration is not a problem to be solved; it is the sign of a successful nation. New Americans are not to be feared as strangers; they are to be welcomed as neighbors.

—George W. Bush
Forty-third President of the
United States

When I first came to America from the Soviet Union, I felt the spirit of freedom everywhere. To think, I could leave the airport and go anyplace I wanted! Smiling and friendliness were everywhere. Even though my English was poor, people tried to understand me, unlike other places I've been where they think you are stupid and ignore you. I was impressed by the American appreciation for diversity, how you don't have to conform to a single standard of beauty. I felt profound gratitude for the opportunity to change profession, the willingness of people to accept me and give me an opportunity to begin a new career. I am a citizen now. I love being an American.

—Sara Lapushner
New York, New York

My father and mother sacrificed everything for our ability to be free.
People died for it. I don't take it for granted.

                    —Andy Garcia, American actor

## From Vietnam War Widow to American Activist
### BY JACKIE BONG-WRIGHT

As a widow of thirty-four I had to flee my country when the northern Communists took over Saigon, South Vietnam, at the end of April 1975. Armed
only with a carry-on bag, a twenty-dollar bill, and the protection of my three
young children—twins of ten and a son of eight—I came to America. Once
here I had to survive the challenges that come with radical change.

At the start, for example, I had to overcome the shame of being labeled
a "parolee," which my dictionary told me was "a person who has been released from prison on parole," but which was stamped on the government-
issued card that was my only ID. I soon learned that "parolee" also means a
person allowed into the United States who does not fit under another cate-
gory. Eventually I married, was naturalized an American, changed my name,
settled in Falls Church, Virginia, and cast my first vote. Gradually, everything
changed. I no longer felt like a second-class citizen. That is because in this
country the conditions for success are all in place.

My first Western lesson: to maximize those conditions, be assertive.
Once you understand that this is all right, the sky's the limit.

Today I am the president and CEO of the Vietnamese American Voters'
Association, Inc. (VAVA), a nonprofit organization providing civic, health,
and education services to Vietnamese Americans. I collaborate with other
immigrant organizations and the League of Women Voters in registering
Vietnamese Americans to vote and organizing candidates' forums. In this
way I help other new Americans take part in the political process. Together
we exercise our responsibilities and choose people to represent our interests
and defend our rights. We show concretely that we can empower ourselves
and are equal to other Americans.

I am one of the two million Vietnamese who have come to these shores since
1975, when Saigon fell to the North Vietnamese communists and the U.S.

government evacuated more than a hundred thousand of us and then, by conscious design, placed us all over the country. That is why even today, although the biggest concentrations of Vietnamese Americans are to be found in California, Texas, and the Washington, D.C., area, you will still find us in every state in the Union.

We are also proud to count ourselves part of the country's 11 million Asian Americans.

Equality is one thing and opportunity often another. That was my second lesson in this country. I had to fight hard for my first job. Employers in the Washington, D.C., area all seemed to want someone who already had experience working in the United States. Not only could I not start out anywhere near the high position I had achieved in South Vietnam, but I couldn't type either. Still, after a lot of discouragement, I finally found something suitable.

And once I stepped through that door, I was on my way. I got training, and I got promoted. I learned that for a hardworking person, there is lots of potential. At thirty-eight I founded my own voluntary agency, set up a temporary shelter for Indochinese refugees, and got federal and state funds to resettle them and find them jobs. At forty-two, I went back to school to earn a master's degree at Georgetown University. At sixty, I became a reporter for a newspaper. This year, I published my memoirs, *Autumn Cloud,* and now I can read about myself and my book on amazon.com!

As for my children, who spoke no English when they first arrived here, they eventually went to Duke, Bryn Mawr, and Yale. My two boys are now working for big corporations in New York, and my daughter is a full-time mother in California.

The third element that struck me about the United States was that the law really works here. Everyone has to take it seriously. I found out the hard way, for example, that people who disregard the speed limit and let parking meters run out pay a penalty, no matter who they are.

But the law frees and protects, too. To me that meant above all being free of Vietnam's communist regime. In America I knew I did not have to worry about being sent out to a barren "new economic zone" or consigned to a "reeducation" camp or a prison cell, the fate of hundreds of thousands of South Vietnamese during the first ten years of my time here.

My older brother was not so fortunate. Falsely accused of being a CIA agent, he died in prison near the capital, Hanoi, after three years of brutal treat-

Jackie Bong-Wright and husband Lacy Wright with President and Mrs. Carter: "I'm proud to be one of 11 million Asian Americans."

ment. He had served twelve years in the South Vietnamese army, taught Vietnamese in Texas at a U.S. government–run language school, and returned to Vietnam the year before the Communist victory. Since he had done nothing wrong, there was no proof of his "crime," and no trial.

I know that that kind of thing cannot happen to me in the United States. I feel secure here.

Finally, it is the spirit of volunteerism and civic participation that flourishes in the United States that makes me especially proud to be an American. Rich or poor, Americans belong to service organizations, neighborhood watch groups, and support teams. Thousands of private foundations fund humanitarian projects, do research, or give directly to the poor. Unlike most people elsewhere who are willing to help only their family and their friends, Americans instinctively see the big picture. They help one another because it is the right and necessary thing to do.

Of course, there are plenty of things that could be improved in the United States. As an Asian woman, speaking with an accent, I have not always been treated in the way I would like. And efforts to strengthen security precautions after the terrible attacks on the World Trade Center have caused legitimate concern among ethnic minorities across the country that their rights may not be honored.

You need, however, to have some perspective. I have lived through a war that saw the assassination of my first husband, a political leader whose car was blown up by the communists in Saigon in 1971. With my second husband, an American diplomat, I have lived in six different countries. During much of my career, I have worked with immigrants. I know from all these experiences that the United States' virtues far outweigh its faults.

That is why people keep coming here from every corner of the world. And that is the ultimate proof that there is no place like America.

**Jackie Bong-Wright** is the author of *Autumn Cloud: From Vietnamese War Widow to American Activist.* She and her husband, Lacy, live in the Washington, D.C., area.

In my dark kitchen I bow my head to pray for strength—for India, facing, on her fiftieth anniversary of freedom, the severe challenges of poverty and illiteracy and communal violence. And for us all, children of the Indian diaspora, here on the other side of the world, who have our own challenges. I pray that we may be able to preserve the values we've gained from our past: love of family, of traditions, of spirituality and the simple life. That we may combine them with what we've learned in our new home: energy and enterprise and how to fight for our rights. This, perhaps, is the best legacy we can leave our children: the art of being Indian-American.

—Chitra Divakaruni, American poet
and novelist, salon.com

I like being an American because in our city in the year 2002 we elected a Hmong woman to the state legislature. She left Cambodia a refugee at the age of nine and in just a little over two decades has made her way into the mainstream of our political system. Only in America can she, an immigrant, and I, a fourth-generation American, achieve such diverse accomplishments without governmental restraint. She developed a voice to represent herself and her constituency. I became an inventor contributing thought and product to the various communities that I touch. America is a privileged place, incredibly human (think Enron) with occasional moments of divinely inspired achievement (think Hmong legislator).

—Charles Girsch
Minneapolis, Minnesota

## Why I'm Glad This Is a Nation of Immigrants
### BY CRYSTAL UVALLE

*It was about twenty years ago.*
*A man came here from Mexico.*
*He sought a better way to live,*
*And found he had a lot to give.*
*He didn't speak a word of English,*
*So he took a job busing dishes.*
*To learn his country's new ways,*
*He worked and studied every day.*
*He made Dallas his new home,*
*And before he knew it he was in the know.*
*He worked his way up in that restaurant,*
*And a lady there, his eye she caught.*
*She was a native of another state,*
*And he asked her out on a date.*
*She liked pierogies and roast beef,*
*He liked tamales and spicy meat.*
*It didn't take long, they were in love,*
*Then God sent them a baby from heaven above.*
*I'm so happy for them you see,*
*That man and woman and I make three.*
*I'm so happy America let him in,*
*He's my father and my friend.*
*I love you, Daddy!*

**Crystal Uvalle** of St. Angela Merici School in White Oak, Pennsylvania, won the American Immigration Law Foundation's Creative Writing Contest for Fifth-Graders with this poem in 1999.

One of the pleasures and perils of including my e-mail address (zakaria@newsweek.com) in my stories is that people use it. Mostly it's a pleasure. But every now and then I get an angry note from someone who adds with ferocious pride that he is a native-born American ("and proud of it!" the last such missive thundered). The idea is that with my "foreign-sounding" name I could not understand the true patriotism of a son of the soil. Actually, it's the other way around. Native-born Americans don't understand an immigrant's love of country. "After all," I've thought of writing back, "what did you do to become an American, other than happen to be born here?" For us immigrants, becoming American was a choice, marked by sorrowful partings and tough new beginnings.

What keeps an immigrant going is faith in his new country. This might not always look like patriotism because it doesn't take the familiar forms—Fourth of July picnics, the fluttering of the Stars and Stripes. Instead it's likely to show itself in a quiet dedication to work, family, and friends. But this is the oldest form of American patriotism—a belief that in this New World you can make your own new world.

Alone among the great civilizations, this country embodies the simple idea of making a better life. Other cultures celebrate military conquests, religious devotion, and ideological grandeur. America celebrates the suburban home with a two-car garage. Jefferson's phrase, "the pursuit of happiness," is our distinctive contribution to humankind.

—Fareed Zakaria, American editor
*Newsweek*


I have a different background. I talk different. Native-born Americans just have to look at me or listen to me and they are reminded of the differences. My goal is to lead a life of righteousness, to conduct myself with honor, to let those other Americans know that I am as good a citizen as I can be.

—Hakeem Olajuwon, Houston
Rockets all-star, the *Houston Chronicle*


Why is the idea of America still so attractive to millions of would-be immigrants around the world?

The conventional answer is that immigrants come to America for one reason: to get rich. The critics of America love this explanation because it attributes the appeal of America to greed and avarice. But as an immigrant, I believe that this notion of what attracts us to America is very limited. It is so limited as to be a distortion.

The distortion works, of course, because there is a molecule of truth in the argument. America does offer a greater degree of social mobility than any other society. Moreover, America provides an incredibly good life for the ordinary guy. Rich people live well everywhere. But in this country, I am constantly struck by how well the common man lives. This is a society where poor people have TVs and microwave ovens. A friend of mine has been trying to relocate to America for years. Finally, I asked him why. He said, "Because I really want to move to a country where the poor people are fat."

Still, the material explanation only partly accounts for the attraction of America to immigrants and to people around the world. Not long ago, I asked myself this question: How would my life have been different if I had never come to America? I grew up in a middle-class family in Bombay. I didn't have luxuries, but neither did I lack for necessities. Materially, my life is better in America, but it is not a fundamental difference. My life has changed far more dramatically in other ways.

If I had stayed in India, I would probably have lived my whole life within a five-mile radius of where I was born. I would undoubtedly have married a girl of my identical socioeconomic and religious background. I would almost certainly have become a doctor, an engineer, or a computer programmer. I would have had a range of political and social opinions that could be predicted in advance.

In many countries in the world, your destiny is, to a large degree, given to you. In America, by contrast, you get to write the script of your own life. I discovered this at Dartmouth, where I became interested in politics, changed my major, and decided to become a writer. I ended up working in the Reagan White House even though I was not a U.S. citizen. I married a woman whose ancestry is English, French, Scotch-Irish, and German. I am one of many immigrants who have discovered that in America, the future is a landscape of our own choosing.

Where to live? How to make our living? Whom to marry? What to believe?

These are questions that, in America, I decide for myself.

It is this notion of being in control of your own life that is the main source of America's appeal around the world, especially to the young. That's why so many people want to come to America and become Americans. Not because this is a place to get rich, but mainly because it is a place where you are the architect of your own destiny.

—Dinesh D'Souza, American author
on *All Things Considered*

Physically Americans were pioneers; in the realm of social and economic institutions, too, their tradition has been one of pioneering. . . . From the beginning Americans have known that there were new worlds to conquer, new truths to be discovered. Every effort to confine Americanism to a single pattern . . . is disloyalty to everything that is valid in Americanism.

—Henry Steele Commager
American historian
*Freedom, Loyalty, and Dissent*

# What Do These Famous People Have in Common?

*Answers on page 55*

# Answers

All of them are Americans, and all of them came from somewhere else. They are among the countless immigrants who have made America what it is today.

Row One: Movie stars Greta Garbo (Sweden); Cary Grant (England); and Audrey Hepburn (Belgium)

Row Two: Football legend Knute Rockne (Norway); baseball hero Sammy Sosa (Dominican Republic); and ballet star Mikhail Baryshnikov (Russia)

Row Three: Novelist Isabel Allende (Chile); model Iman (Somalia); and musician Carlos Santana (Mexico)

Row Four: Saint Mother Cabrini (Italy); scientist Albert Einstein (Germany); and businessman An Wang, as in Wang Laboratories (Korea)

Other famous immigrants include the first Secretary of the Treasury, Alexander Hamilton (British West Indies); former Secretaries of State Henry Kissinger (Germany) and Madeleine Albright (Czechoslovakia); former U.S. Senator Lowell Weicker (France) and U.S. Navy Admiral Hyman Rickover (Poland); strongman Charles Atlas (Italy) and gentle gymnast Nadia Comenici (Romania); poet Kahlil Gibran (Lebanon) and memoirist Frank McCourt (Ire-

Madeleine Albright, first woman Secretary of State

land); basketball star Hakeem Olajuwon (Nigeria) and tennis champion Martina Navratilova (Czech Republic); comic actors Bob Hope (England) and Dan Aykroyd (Canada); Academy Award winners Sidney Poitier (Bahamas) and Julie Andrews (England); Grammy Award winner Gloria Estefan (Cuba) and opera singer Plácido Domingo (Spain); architect I. M. Pei (China) and telephone inventor Alexander Graham Bell (Scotland)—to name a few. To learn more about notable American immigrants, check out immigration.about.com/cs/famous-immigrants or ailf.org/notable/famous.htm.

> I have loved being an American, and now being able to be a part of American history is an unparalleled honor. And I guess everybody is a patriotic American, but I have to tell you that those who weren't born here have an extra stripe of patriotism, I do believe.
> —Madeleine Albright
> former U.S. Secretary of State
> born in Czechoslovakia

# Chapter Four

# THE AMERICAN SPIRIT

I am certain that after the dust of centuries has passed from our cities, we will be remembered not for victories or defeats in battle or politics, but for our contributions to the human spirit.

—John F. Kennedy
Thirty-fifth President of the
United States

What then is the spirit of liberty? I cannot define it; I can only tell you my own faith. The spirit of liberty is the spirit which is not too sure that it is right. The spirit of liberty is the spirit which seeks to understand the minds of other men and women. The spirit of liberty is the spirit which weighs their interests alongside its own without bias. The spirit of liberty remembers that not even a sparrow falls to earth unheeded. The spirit of liberty is the spirit of Him whom, near two thousand years ago, taught mankind that lesson it has never learned, but has never quite forgotten; that there may be a kingdom where the least shall be heard and considered side by side with the greatest.

—Supreme Court Justice
Learned Hand

Our United States has a corporate personality, a spirit, a soul. To partake of this great American experiment is sheer grace.

—Bishop Robert Morneau
Green Bay, Wisconsin

## The Spirit of the Constitution and Declaration of Independence

BY EMMET FOX

The United States is not merely one more nation added to the list of nationalities. It stands for certain special ideas and special principles which have never been definitely expressed in concrete form in the world before. These ideas may be summed up in the conception of personal freedom and unlimited opportunity.

What may be called the American Spirit is an intangible though very real thing in itself, but as far as it can be put into words it has been expressed in the two great official documents of the American Republic, namely, the Constitution and Declaration of Independence.

These two documents are among the most remarkable ever written, and their effect upon the history of the world has probably never been surpassed. They are both quite short, not more than a few thousand words in length, but every thoughtful man anywhere, and certainly every American, should make himself acquainted with them.

The first things that strike us in considering these documents is the remarkable difference in their approach to the subject. The Constitution contains no direct preaching at all. It makes no direct statements about the nature of man or his destiny, or of man's relations with other people or with God. It is, seemingly, just a dry legal document. Never does it say in so many words that man should be free, that human beings should live together in brotherhood, or that man is the child of God. All these things are expressed or implied in the Declaration of Independence; and the Declaration is, I suppose, one of the most vivid and colorful documents that has ever been written. It thrills with hope and faith and enthusiasm. The Constitution, on the other hand, is formal, technical, precise, and not, at first sight, of any interest to the layman. Indeed, the Constitution and the Declaration might be described, in a sense, as the anatomy and physiology of government—the one concerned with the hard dry bones of the supporting skeleton, and the other with the warm living organs and tissues of life.

To understand the American Constitution one must realize that it aims at bringing about a definitely selected condition of things. It aims at a special way of life—a way of life that up to the present has only been found in completeness in the United States. It aims at *personal freedom* for the individual. It aims at the idea of substantial equality, and above all, at equality of opportunity. No civilization had ever before aimed at that. The great Roman Empire had certain magnificent aims, but equality of opportunity was not one of them. The Greek civilization had wonderful aims, but they did not include that. Glorious Athens was always based on a foundation of slavery. The Middle Ages definitely rejected the idea of personal freedom and equality of opportunity, and aimed rather at discipline and uniformity.

America is the land of opportunity.

The American Constitution makes certain assumptions about the average man. It assumes that the average man is a sensible sort of fellow. It assumes that he is honest, and it assumes that he is good-natured. You say, "Well, of course, that is natural." Once more I tell you it is not a matter of course. All the previous civilizations were based on exactly the opposite assumptions. All the polities of the ancient world, and of the Middle Ages in particular, were founded on the idea that the average man is naturally foolish; and that unless he is watched and controlled and regimented and scared half out of his wits, he will get into mischief and damage himself or other people in some way. They assumed that he is dishonest. They assumed that he is extremely selfish, and is usually actuated by the lowest motives. Of course, these statements were never written down anywhere. Statesmen do not write such things—such things do not look well in writing. But they wrote other things down, in technical and diplomatic language, that were based on exactly the premises that I have stated. Only in this Constitution is it assumed that the average man is to be trusted. Now it is easy to see why the Constitution calls definitely for *personal initiative, personal self-reliance, personal common sense,* and a disposition to compromise sensibly where there cannot be complete agreement; and why it cannot work without these things.

Stupid people sometimes say that the American Spirit is an absurd ideal because men are essentially unequal. The local electrician, they point out, is not the equal of Edison; and Emerson was not the equal of the man who groomed his horse. Of course, the authors of the Constitution were perfectly aware of this fact, and it is precisely this fact which they had in mind when the Constitution was designed by them. In a free country, equality means equality of opportunity to make the most of one's talents; and equality before the law, which must not discriminate between one citizen and

July 8, 1776: The first public reading of the Declaration of Independence. PAINTING BY
LOUIS S. GLANZMAN

another. It means the absence of special privilege of any kind, under any pretense.

The Declaration of Independence does not say that men are *born* free and equal, because they are not so born. It says, *"created* equal"—quite a different thing. Of course, we are all born different. It is equality of opportunity that matters, and it is equality of opportunity that the Constitution sets out to produce. Now we see that in this way, in this seemingly dry legal document, these inspired men were producing a general model for human government. Sooner or later the rest of the world will adopt the principles of the American Constitution. Human nature being what it is, each people or nation will probably call it its own constitution, but it will essentially be the American Constitution, and it does not matter at all what they call it as long as they put it into effect.

The Constitution has amply justified itself. It has given the people the highest standard of living in the world. The poorest people in the United States are still better off than the poor in any other country. In spite of eight or nine years of depression panic—and it is only a panic of fear—in spite of other difficulties, there is still a higher standard of living in this country than in any other. And the next highest standard, note carefully, is in the other free countries. It is in the countries where freedom and the rights of the individual have been trampled underfoot that the lowest general standard of living prevails.

The Constitution has produced the greatest educational opportunities. There are more opportunities for education in this country, particularly for the poor boy or girl, than in any place in the world. There are more chances for success and self-realization, and for prosperity and happiness for the average man in this country than anywhere else. . . .

Such, in broad outline, is the spirit of the American Constitution, and I, for one, am proud to pay my personal tribute to the lofty vision and the practical statesmanship it embodies.

**Emmet Fox,** who came to the United States from England, wrote these words in 1939. He was one of the most popular and influential spiritual leaders of the twentieth century and the author of many books, including *The Sermon on the Mount* and *Alter Your Life,* from which this essay comes.

With the Declaration, Jefferson gave the Enlightenment its most eloquent and succinct political expression. He lifted the human race into a higher orbit.

—Lance Morrow

American essayist, *Time* magazine

The Constitution of the United States, the Bill of Rights. Just saying these words conjures up a sense of authority, a sense of security, the tenets by which we live our lives. The foundation of our society, of our freedom, can be found within the pages of these documents. Although we may not think of the Bill of Rights every day, it is comforting to know that it is always there, offering protection and liberty for each and every American.

—Dr. Joyce Brothers

American psychologist

The first ten amendments to the Constitution were ratified December 15, 1791, and form what is known as the Bill of Rights. Together they put bite into the spirit of freedom and justice found in the Declaration. Here is a taste, together with observations from people who care.

*Congress shall make no law respecting an establishment of religion, or prohibiting the free exercise thereof; or abridging the freedom of speech, or of the press, or the right of the people peaceably to assemble, and to petition the government for a redress of grievances.*

—The First Amendment

Whenever I pick up a newspaper and read about someone in another nation being imprisoned for writing a critical or even semi-critical article about the leader of that country, I am grateful for the freedoms which we have in our nation under the First Amendment. When I read about Christians and Falun Gong adherents being executed in China, I count my blessings. But I also know that self-restraint is needed. Excesses such as movie and TV violence that strain the outer boundaries of the First Amendment can endanger our basic freedom by stirring interest in government censorship. As a former newspaper publisher, U.S. congressman and senator, and as a lifelong churchgoer, I hope that the entertainment media will exercise the responsibility and self-discipline that our beautiful First Amendment freedom requires from each of us.

—Paul Simon

Carbondale, Illinois

*In all criminal prosecutions, the accused shall enjoy the right to a speedy and public trial, by an impartial jury . . . and to be informed of the nature and cause of the accusation; to be confronted with the witnesses against him; to have compulsory process for obtaining witnesses in his favor, and to have the assistance of counsel for his defense.*

—The Sixth Amendment

I am a criminal defense lawyer. I remember walking out of a dingy overcrowded criminal court one afternoon with my seventeen-year-old client, Juan. He had testified in his own case and someone else had testified in contradiction to everything he had said. After a brief cross-examination of the officer, the judge had ruled in our favor.

Later in the hall, Juan turned to me and asked, "Mr. Reardon, was I under oath in there?"

"Yes," I said.

"Did that mean I had to tell the honest truth?"

"Yes," I said, a little afraid of what I would hear next.

But then Juan went on. "Mr. Reardon, didn't that witness take the same oath?"

I had no answer for my young client then or now, except to say that I like living in a place where a seventeen-year-old inner-city kid can have a chance to be believed when he swears to tell the truth. People seek my help when all have turned against them and they feel the withering stares of accusation and the self-doubt such looks breed. I like living in a country where I can walk with these accused into the highest forums in the land and demand that they be presumed innocent as their right.

> —Patrick Reardon
> Chicago, Illinois

*Neither slavery nor involuntary servitude, except as a punishment for crime whereof the party shall have been duly convicted, shall exist within the United States, or any place subject to their jurisdiction.*

> —The Thirteenth Amendment. Proposed
> by Congress on January 31, 1865, and
> declared ratified on December 6, 1865

At the beginning of the World Series of 1947, I experienced a completely new emotion when the National Anthem was played. This time, I thought, it is being played for me, as much as for anyone else. This is organized major league baseball, and I am standing here with all the others; and everything that takes place includes me.

> —Jackie Robinson, the first African-
> American to play on a major league
> baseball team

*The right of citizens of the United States to vote shall not be denied or abridged by the United States or by any State on account of sex.*

> —The Nineteenth Amendment. Pro-
> posed by Congress on June 4, 1919,
> and declared ratified on
> August 18, 1920

I can do anything, because everything is allowed.
                    —Meryl Streep, American actress

All my life I've been here. It is difficult to imagine what life would be like without the freedoms I take for granted—if I had to worry about what I say, what I do, or even what I think. Sure, things aren't perfect, the system doesn't always work, but the spirit is here, and everything has the potential to work. Life, liberty, and the pursuit of happiness are our mantras. They focus our lives whether we know it or not. When we read the newspapers and see how people in many other countries live, we begin to see how precious our basic values are. Though I moan and complain about things American, I am grateful to be here and wouldn't have it any other way.
                    —Matthew Laughlin
                    Brooklyn, New York


We live in an age of science and of abounding accumulation of material things. These did not create our Declaration. Our Declaration created them. The things of the spirit come first.
                    —Calvin Coolidge
                    Thirtieth President of the
                    United States


America did not invent human rights. In a very real sense human rights invented America.
                    —Jimmy Carter
                    Thirty-ninth President of the
                    United States


My pride in being American relates to the long tradition of American dissent. There is a particular combination of orneriness, openheartedness, and vision that I think of as distinctly American. Less intellectually sophisticated than the European socialist tradition to be sure, less historically minded than the English, often less ready to face violent repression than the brave souls who fight for justice in Latin

America or Asia. But from Thoreau and Rachel Carson to Eugene Debs and Noam Chomsky, from the enormous inventiveness of the American women who created modern feminism to the rank and file of the environmental movement, there is an American spirit that refuses to accept injustice, degradation, and senseless loss. At its best this spirit combines political critique with a simple love of life (as in Dorothy Day), a rejection of injustice with a simple celebration of community and the natural world (as in Bill McKibben). This tradition inspires, enlightens, and gives us all something to live up to.

—Roger S. Gottlieb
Worcester, Massachusetts

I like being a member of this fractured community that continually mends itself. We keep working toward resolving the tension between our enshrined ideals and our flawed execution of them. We're a community that wants to acknowledge its mistakes, correct them, and move onward with hope. That's the American spirit. And besides, where else in the world can you get a whole wheat, pineapple, ham pizza? Talk about inclusive!

—Frank Cunningham
Notre Dame, Indiana

I love living in a country filled with a spirit of optimism. In World War II we were attacked and had to fight for our lives against Japan and Germany. Within a few years we were giving them a hand up. Within a generation we were friends. You can only do that if you're an optimist and think: That was then, and this is now. Things were bad then, but we'll make things turn out better this time. We are willing to put history behind us, where it belongs, and look forward. That's the American spirit.

—Mark Geimer
Greenwich, Connecticut

Yesterday my daughter asked me, "Mom, why do you like being an American?" Now, I am eighty years old, so I had to think about it, and think and remember I did.

I guess I always took being an American for granted. I was born here and lived here all my life. I have always been able to practice my faith freely in the church of my choice, speak and be heard if I wasn't pleased about something, and vote for whomever I wanted.

I lived through prosperity, a terrible Depression, and prosperity again. I can remember my dad having a good job with good pay one year and the next year being almost penniless and asking me to pray for snow so he could get a job shoveling for the city. (There were no plows then.)

Those were rough times, but we got through them, just like our country has done many times. As the song says,

*Pick yourself up, dust yourself off, and start all over again!*

America is the land of new beginnings. Americans always rally around each other in times of tragedy. I remember seeing friends I grew up with go off to World War II, and some of them never came home. But somehow the families of those boys pulled through with the help of those around them. Now I know families who lost loved ones in the World Trade Center on September 11, and we are losing more young people in the war on terrorism. But I am proud of the way Americans are coming together once more to support each other. With God's help I know we will begin again.

—Agnes Gaughan
Bronx, New York

## The American Spirit in Action
BY DICK COLT

On September 13, 2001, I stood in front of the ruins of the World Trade Center. I came to the site as the Commanding General of ten thousand Army Reserve soldiers in New York and New Jersey. I came with key members of my staff to assess the support we could give to New York City in the rescue and recovery operations under way. I found both a national tragedy and the triumph of the American spirit. I found another reason to be extraordinarily proud of Americans and to be so thankful that I am an American.

We had walked down to the site from 26 Federal Plaza, approximately eight blocks. As we neared Ground Zero we found ash everywhere. The smell of fire and plumes of smoke were ever present. There was no traffic and no pedestrians moved except those like us, on a mission. My first sight of the smoking, smoldering ruins brought a feeling of horror and pain. I knew that at least six of my citizen soldiers were buried in the rubble. I didn't know how many others were lost. I'd seen the pictures but being there was so much worse. I couldn't believe that it was real. This couldn't have happened. The site was as quiet as an open-air cathedral. I was aware of the determined grinding of machinery, but human speech was muted and when heard, spoken in soft eye-to-eye contacts.

Five or six hundred people were working throughout the area. Rescue workers clambered over piles of wreckage. Cranes with huge claws lifted steel beams to clear access for rescue vehicles. Volunteers provided sustenance to rescue workers. Organized chaos reigned. Then the American Express Building, which was on the south side of the wreckage field, groaned as if in pain. Immediately everyone near that building turned on their heels and raced to where we were standing a block away. There was no panic, no screaming, and no desperation. Everyone then turned and watched the building until the eerie sounds ceased. We watched and waited for whatever would happen next. Ten minutes later nothing had happened, and these great people moved back toward the ruins and back to work. My team went with them. As we walked in I knew that the building could come down and so did all the folks serving there. Yet they entered with a purpose and a commitment I can truthfully say was awesome to behold. The quiet courage of regular Americans was on display for all to see.

Major General Dick Colt (*left*) with Sergeant Major Kenneth Esposito. "America is the place where how we look, pray, talk, or believe is not what binds us together. We are bound together in a multi-generation endeavor to achieve the goals crafted in our Declaration of Independence and solidified in our Constitution."

As we moved through the area I looked around at all the men and women working to rescue their brothers and sisters. Young to old, in uniforms of every type and in civilian clothes of every stripe, short to tall, every flesh tone conceivable, multiple languages heard, every cultural heritage and faith of our people, I have no doubt, present for duty. I felt then, and still feel now, that all that is good in America shone in the weary faces of those wonderful heroes. Those who attacked us, who disguised their motives in a false rendering of the messages of a great and gentle religion, Islam, have no idea of the American spirit. They didn't realize that by attacking America, they killed many wonderful people but they allowed us to demonstrate the great values of courage, self-sacrifice, compassion, commitment to others, and honor. They hurt us, but gave us heroes who reflect the great spectrum of the American rainbow and embody the American spirit.

I was not born here. My mother, and several of her sisters, worked in an ammunition factory in Scotland during World War II. My father was an Army Air Corps sergeant stationed within bicycling distance. His brothers were in uniform around the world. In February 1946 I came to America as one of the first war babies brought here after war's end. I was five months old. Two years later my dad sponsored my mother's family and brought representatives of three generations of Scots to America. My heritage is one of service to God and country.

I started life in America on the Lower East Side of New York and then, as generations of new Americans had done, moved to the open environments of the Bronx. I became the first college graduate in my father's line. After service in Vietnam I became our family's first white-collar manager, and when I was promoted to major, the highest-ranking officer in my family's history. Last year at the age of fifty-six I was promoted to the rank of major general. I write these words not for self-glorification, but to illustrate why I love America, why I'm so very proud to be an American, and why the American spirit means so much to me.

America is the place where dreams can come true, where opportunity is waiting for those who seek it, where anything you dream can be made real. There is no place in the world where I believe "hope" is as fundamental a word as it is here. America is the place where desire, hard work, and luck can overcome most obstacles.

My military service has given me continuous examples of American dreams fulfilled. One of my commanders in Vietnam was the son of a Mississippi River fisherman. He went to Howard University, graduated as an Army officer, and became one of the finest leaders I have been privileged to serve with. He taught me leadership skills I still use today. I've seen countless young men and women, possessing great street survival skills and minimal self-discipline, learn their strengths, overcome their weaknesses, and move on to become great citizens in every sense of the word. I've slept in foxholes and tents with soldiers from every walk of life and tradition. I've learned from every one of them. I've buried friends with honor guards of every cultural tradition proudly folding our Stars and Stripes in front of grieving families, and heard Taps played over men and women who served America on liberty's ramparts. I've watched the back of people of every color and they have protected mine.

I've observed Christmas, Kwanzaa, Hanukkah, St. Patrick's Day, Ramadan, Columbus Day, and a multitude of cultural traditions with my soldiers. I've been an honorary and a real godfather to soldiers' children. I've been with them, and they with me, through the dark, hard times when shoulders are to lean on, regardless of the skin color under the uniform. I've learned that the common bond of our humanity, the strength of our hearts, the values displayed and the deeds of our lives, and the goodness of our souls are the true measure of a man or woman. I've grown to middle age with a United Nations' worth of American comrades and am all the better for it.

Where else in this troubled world could I have experienced the great joys of a life unfettered by rigid caste lines, or religious intolerance, or societal constraints? Where else but in America could a kid off a boat have the life I have led? Where else could the rainbow hues that are my friends and family be able to gather without fear of persecution?

Where else can we air our grievances, petty to great, and not fear a nocturnal visit by the authorities? Where else in the world are people still fleeing *to* in the hope of a better life for them and their family? Where else could the four great freedoms—"freedom from want, freedom of speech, freedom of religion, and freedom from fear"—be cornerstones of a society?

America is the place where how we look, pray, talk, or believe is not what binds us together. Rather we are bound by a vision enunciated by another hero, Dr. Martin Luther King, Jr., in his eternal "I Have a Dream" speech. We are bound together in a multigeneration endeavor to achieve the goals crafted in our Declaration of Independence and solidified in our Constitution. We strive together to reconcile our human failings with the wonderful goal of individual freedom and collective responsibility for each other. We journey together from sea to shining sea toward that "bright light on the hill" that is the spirit of America realized.

We're not there yet but, bottom line, I like being American because it's taken me on a life's journey with almost 300 million other Americans toward the achievement of the greatest of all human conditions—freedom and liberty for all. I may not be around when we get there but the trip is surely wonderful. It is the American spirit in action.

Do I just like being an American? No, I love being an American.

**Dick Colt**, a major general in the U.S. Army Reserves and a successful businessman, lives in Ossining, New York.

My parents raised two children to whom they gave a precious gift, a set of core beliefs. A value system founded on a clear understanding of the difference between right and wrong and a belief in the Almighty. They taught us integrity, kindness, and Godliness were right. Lying, violence, intolerance, crime, and drugs were wrong, and, even worse than wrong, they were shameful. In my family we were taught that hard work and education were the keys to success. My sister and I were taught to believe in ourselves. We might be considered poor, but we were rich in spirit. But, stick with it, because in America, justice will eventually triumph and the powerful, searing promise of the founding fathers will

Abraham Lincoln with Sojourner Truth, former slave and human rights advocate

come true. We were taught by my parents to always, always, always believe in America.

—Colin Powell
U.S. Secretary of State

I have never had a feeling politically that did not spring from the Declaration of Independence. . . . I have often inquired of myself what great principle it was that kept this confederacy so long together. It was not the mere matter of the separation of the colonies from the mother land, but something in that Declaration giving liberty, not alone to the people of this country, but hope for the world for all future time. It was that which gave promise that in due time the weights should be lifted from the shoulders of all men, and that all should have an equal chance. This is the sentiment, embodied in the Declaration of Independence.

I would rather be assassinated on the spot than surrender it.

—Abraham Lincoln
Sixteenth President of the
United States

## The American Woman

If I were asked . . . to what the singular prosperity and growing strength of the American people ought mainly to be attributed, I should reply: To the superiority of their women.

> —Alexis de Tocqueville, *Democracy in America* (1840)

You must do the thing you think you cannot do.

> —Eleanor Roosevelt, American stateswoman

I did everything Fred Astaire did—backwards, and in heels.

> —Ginger Rogers, American dancer

One can never consent to creep when one feels an impulse to soar.

> —Helen Keller, American inspiration

My mother wanted me to be her wings, to fly as she never quite had the courage to do. I love her for that. I love the fact that she wanted to give birth to her own wings.

> —Erica Jong, American novelist

Mothers of the race [are] the most important actors in the grand drama of human progress.

> —Elizabeth Cady Stanton
> American reformer

# AMERICAN SOUL

In God We Trust

—U.S. motto on currency

We have staked the whole future of the American civilization not upon the power of government, far from it. We have staked the whole future . . . upon the capacity of each and all of us to govern ourselves, to control ourselves, to sustain ourselves according to the Ten Commandments of God.

—James Madison
Fourth President of the
United States

Behold how good and pleasant it is when brothers dwell in unity!

—Judaism

We are members one of another.

—Christianity

Abu Musa reported the Prophet as saying, "Believers are to one another like a building whose parts support one another." He then interlaced his fingers.

—Islam

## An American Muslim Looks Back with Love

### BY ASMA GULL HASAN

The invitation to the wedding should have read:

*You are Cordially Invited*
*To a Wedding in the South*
*With an Atheist Bride*
*And Her Muslim and Taiwanese Bridesmaids—*
*First Methodist Church,*
*Louisville, Kentucky*

It would have been accurate. The actual invitation never indicated a wedding that reflected the face of America. But the wedding did.

I remember how proudly we stood on that hot August day in the cavernous church—three women who shared a college education and, to the naked eye, little else. I remember discreetly slipping off my Payless-dyed shoes and hiding them under the long hem of my polyester baby-blue gown, adorned with a gigantic blue satin bow. I looked at Isabel, the Taiwanese bridesmaid, and shared a silent chuckle with her.

We had been up since nine a.m.—curling our hair, keeping Amy from crying over her groom's bachelor-night sojourn to a strip club, squeezing into her mom's car with the maid of honor (her sister), and pulling Amy's parachute-like white dress over her smiling face in the church basement. I remember how Isabel and I laid out our own clothes on the Ping-Pong table, trying to decide if we should stand in our underwear until the photographer was ready for the pre-ceremony photographs to avoid sweating all over them.

And I remember how we all became friends.

When I first met Amy in our first year at Wellesley College, all I could tell was that she was shy, white, from the South, and involved in the Campus Crusade for Christ. What was that all about, I wondered? Was it anything like the Crusades I learned about in history? Would I experience a moment when everyone in class, including the teacher, would look at me and ask me to explain the bar-

baric religion of the "Islamics"? Fortunately not, of course, although one class-mate, also a member of Campus Crusade, whom I was close to said to me, "I'm sorry you won't be in the afterlife with me. I'll miss you!"

I often found myself explaining Islam and what real Muslims are like—how we were just like any other group, with mostly good apples and some bad. Some people even said to me, "But how can you be Muslim? I *like* you!"

It was (and still is) my mission in life, my *jihad*, to show people the real face of Islam, long before I ever started studying Islam formally or writing about being an American Muslim. So many things that are second nature or even blasé to me come as a total surprise and epiphany to many non-Muslim Americans. When I explain that Muslims consider Christians and Jews as "Brothers of the Book" because of the similarity between their holy books, their eyes light up. I tell some people how the Qur'an says that all moral religions come from the same source: *God*. The Qur'an, despite some bad press of late, reflects great social reforms. It even says, "O mankind! We created you from a single (pair) of a male and a female, and made you into nations and tribes, that ye may know each other (not that ye may despise each other)." The Qur'an was one of the first multicultural, multifaith, gender-equal proclamations ever.

So when people say to me, "It must be hard for you to be American," I want to laugh. Islam and the American spirit are like siblings in the family of great ideas through time. Muslims are required as a part of their religion to give to charity, just as Americans are expected to give back to their communities. The Qur'an holds no ethnicity or gender higher than another, as the U.S. Constitution also does. I cannot think of anything more American than being Muslim!

The symbol of Islam is the crescent moon and star, not because the Prophet Muhammad (peace be upon him) said so but because Islam bases its calendar on the cycles of the moon—the lunar calendar. The star fits nicely inside the empty dimple of the crescent. The American flag has a similar comfortable asymmetry to it. But I have wondered how such a basic design could come to symbolize so much. I imagine that if I went to a graphic designer today and described the original thirteen colonies and asked her to create our flag, the last thing she would come up with would be today's American flag. Who would put stars and stripes together? A contemporary designer might turn the idea into a gaudy tracksuit: red velour with white stars down the side on a blue tuxedo stripe.

Yet the flag looks beautiful just the way it is; it elegantly symbolizes what makes America so terrific: our *unity in diversity.*

And that's the beautiful secret of how an Asian, a Muslim, and a Southern girl became best friends and celebrated love at an American wedding.

Just like the stars and stripes magically match, my olive skin and black hair mix right in with my white (now atheist) friend and her other bridesmaid, the daughter of Taiwanese immigrants. In what other country could a Muslim be the bridesmaid for a wedding in a Christian church? In what other country could people of such diverse backgrounds be best friends? I love our diversity because, like so much in America, it's a great privilege and a source of both celebration and gratitude.

**Asma Gull Hasan** is the author of *American Muslims: The New Generation.* She lives in Denver, Colorado.

All human creatures are God's children, and those dearest to God are those who treat his children kindly.
—Islam

Have we not all one father? Has not one God created us?
—Judaism

We are made in the image and likeness of God.
—Christianity

An American Jew Appreciates the Present
BY SHMULEY BOTEACH

If the Bible had not specifically named Israel to be "the promised land," the Jews would have to be forgiven for mistaking America for it.

For centuries Jews were forced to exist in time rather than in space. We packed up our lives and our histories and bundled them into our prayers, our studies, and in the great minds of our spiritual leaders. Often, we quite literally carried our lives in large, bulky packs balanced on our backs. We never settled for long, nor had the luxury of making a land of our own, because frankly, nobody much wanted us. Few were willing to tolerate our presence, even if it was just our cemeteries that lingered behind. Then we reached America.

Jews were systematically expelled from nearly every other country they settled in over the last two thousand years. King Edward I expelled us on July 18, 1290, making England the first European country to do so. Spain issued its "Final Edict" in March of 1492, declaring that all Jews must convert to Catholicism or be banished. Portugal was an even messier situation. Following King Joao's death in 1494, Manuel I ascended to the throne. His legitimacy as heir to the throne was questioned, so he decided to crystallize his position by marrying Princess Isabel of Spain. Isabel told Manuel that she would only marry him if he expelled the Jews. Talk about magnanimous wedding presents! Their marriage contract was signed on November 30, 1496, and five days later he issued a decree forcing all Jews to leave Portugal by October 1497. Thus on March 19, 1497, Jewish parents were commanded to take their children to Lisbon. Upon arrival, the parents were informed that their children were going to be taken away from them, to be given to Catholic families and raised as practicing Catholics. The children were literally torn from their parent's arms. Some parents chose to kill themselves and their offspring rather than be separated. Is it any wonder that Jews can feel slightly insecure about the countries they reside in?

True, some nations actually allowed us to stay within their borders. But they did so begrudgingly. In these countries Jews served either as pawns in a subservient state, as in the Papal States, or as nomads moving from one undesirable location to the next, dictated by each new pogrom or murderous rant, as in Russia. Even today in Israel, our true and irreplaceable Promised Land, there is a large faction of the population that views Jews as germs to be eradicated, a feat which has been attempted time and again with car bombs, suicide bombers, public killing sprees, and other terrorist attacks. Needless to say, it has not done wonders for the collective Jewish self-esteem, knowing that no one really wanted us, and at best could bitterly tolerate us.

Then along came one Christopher Columbus and the discovery and exploration of a new uncharted world. (Ironically, this was also the work of Queen Isabel, who had been so instrumental in ridding Europe of Jews in the first place). Interesting to note that among Columbus's expedition party were certainly a few Jews, including one Luis De Torres. Torres led one of the first recorded expeditions into the New World, where he fell in love with the land that is now Cuba (which might explain my own penchant for cigars). He purchased a plot of land and settled there to start a life. His was the first Jewish home in the Americas, but it was not to be the last.

Admittedly though, even in America, Jewish settlement was not an instant reality. We have Rabbi Manasseh Ben Israel of Amsterdam, Holland, to thank for making America a safe ground for Jewish settlement. At the time that colonists began immigrating to the New World, there existed in the books a four-hundred-year-old law forbidding Jews from living on any English-ruled land. That, of course, included the Americas, and was quoted by early American leaders who did not want Jews there, as a deterrent to their pending immigration. Rabbi Manasseh went to meet with Oliver Cromwell and stated emphatically that the law must be declared null and void. If the law remained, he continued, the D-day of Judgment would never arrive because, he quoted from scripture, "Before all prophecies be fulfilled, the people of G-d must first be dispersed into all the places and countries of the world." This was an argument that was difficult to counter, and besides, Cromwell knew that Jews would be good for the economy of the New World. Cromwell conceded and Jewish settlement ensued.

A major factor promoting the success of the Jewish people in America was that, for the first time ever, the ideals of freedom of religion and freedom of the press were put into practice. These two freedoms were essential to the survival of the Jewish people. In the past, a state-controlled press had served as a convenient accomplice to those spreading rumors of blood libel and well poisoning by those ne'er-do-well Jews. When the papers reported such tall tales in a country without freedom of the press, every story published was one-sided. Jews were denied any defense, and anti-Semitism was allowed to spread with germlike rapidity. With the welcome advent of freedom of the press, Jews were finally given a voice of their own. While anti-Semitism did certainly exist at times throughout American history, Jews were never again rendered as helpless as they were in the old country.

Freedom of religion meant that Jews could finally build synagogues and form congregations in their communities. In 1789, President George Washington wrote to the head of Congregation Mickve Israel in Savannah, Georgia, congratulating them on the official opening of a new synagogue:

> *May the same wonder-working Deity who long since delivering*
> *the Hebrews from their Egyptian oppressors, planted them in*
> *the promised land—whose providential agency has lately been*
> *conspicuous in establishing these United States as an independent*
> *nation—still continue to water them with the dews of Heaven*
> *and to make the inhabitants of every denomination participate*
> *in the temporal and spiritual blessing of that people whose God*
> *is Jehovah.*

Jews were now indeed "planted in the promised land," or at least of sorts. For the Jews there could never and will never be any replacement for their ancient homeland in Israel. But that did not stop us for thanking G-d for helping us arrive in a land flowing with milk and honey. And once planted, oh how we grew.

One of the most notable Jewish names in the first hundred years of American history was Judah P. Benjamin, a key member in Jefferson Davis's Confederate cabinet. It is odd to me that a people fighting to uphold the oppression of one minority group, blacks, would allow a Jew to rise so high in their ranks. But to them he was not a Jew; he was merely another American fighting for the Confederacy. Benjamin was nicknamed the "Brains of the Confederacy," serving as attorney general, secretary of war, and finally as secretary of state from March 1862 to the end of the war.

It astounds me that at the same time that a Jew in America was moving up the ranks to a high-ranking government position, Pope Pius IX was quoted as saying, "Before the time of Jesus the Jews had been children in the House of God. But owing to their obstinacy and their failure to believe, they have become dogs. . . . We have today in Rome unfortunately too many of these dogs, and we hear them barking in all the streets, and going around molesting people everywhere." While the world's "spiritual" leaders regarded us as canines, America viewed us as generals, as scholars, as artists, as scientists, as bankers, as philanthropists, as productive citizens, and as equals. Indeed, America viewed us as *human*. And for that, America became the second most loved home of the Jews in all history.

I spent eleven years in Oxford as rabbi to the Jewish students at the university. These were perhaps the most formative years of my life—from twenty-one to thirty-two—and yet I was never a Brit. My voice was too loud, my accent too noticeable, my enthusiasm too unquenchable, my dreams too grand, my aspirations not understated enough. All classic American traits. And the truth is, I never wanted to assimilate. I love this country too much. My wife, who was born in Australia, loves this country too much. My kids love this country too much. Although with only one exception they were all born in Britain, after September 11, they were the ones festooning our house and car with American flags, chastising my wife, Debbie, and me for not having done it already. The United States welcomed us in when everyone else shut their doors. And for that, we are forever Americans. Yes, we are Jews first, but the beauty of America is that that is never a problem or a contradiction.

And it's so great to be an American. I even attended the World Series this year, and Lee Greenwood was there at the beginning of the game singing his classic song "Proud to Be an American." I'm not one for loud public sing-alongs, but I nearly drowned out the rest of the ballpark as I joined with Lee in singing the beautiful words, "I thank my lucky stars that I still live here today, because the flag still stands for freedom, and they can't take that away. . . . There ain't no doubt I love this land, G-d bless the USA."

And I teach my children of the great Americans who fought and died for freedom. I teach them of Abraham Lincoln who, while conducting a civil war, still found the time to remand an order by General Grant banning Jewish merchants from selling wares to the Northern Army. I tell them of President Theodore Roosevelt who issued a stern warning to blood-soaked Russia to stop all pogroms against the Jews or risk permanent diplomatic fallout with the United States. I teach them of President Harry Truman who was the first of the major world leaders to recognize the fledgling State of Israel in 1948. And I teach them too of Richard Nixon who, although he had many unkind things to say of Jews, still responded to Israel's greatest crisis in the Yom Kippur War of 1973 with the greatest military airlift since the Berlin Crisis, and played an instrumental role in saving the Jewish state from Arab annihilation.

And I teach my children to look at the American currency, the greatest symbol of prosperity, where this country had the humility to print, "In G-d We Trust." And I show them in the halls of Congress how the eternal words "E Pluribus Unum" are engraved in stone.

Now, even as I walk the sunlit streets of this beautiful land, I proclaim with all my Jewish heart and soul, "G-d bless America!"

**Rabbi Shmuley Boteach** is director of the L'Chaim Society, New York City, a Jewish education organization that hosts world figures and statesmen lecturing on values-based leadership. He is also the author of a number of books, including *Judaism for Everyone*.

The most beautiful thing a man can do is to forgive wrong.
                                        —Judaism

Forgive thy servants seventy times a day.
                                        —Islam

Then Peter came up and said to him, "Lord, how often shall my brother sin against me, and I forgive him? As many as seven?" Jesus said to him, "I do not say to you seven times, but seventy times seven."

                                        —Christianity

An American Christian Looks Forward with Hope
BY MICHAEL LEACH

I said something smart to my sons once. I hope it wasn't the first time, or the last time. But it was an interesting time. The Berlin Wall had just fallen, in the twinkling of an eye, and we were watching it on TV. I said, "A good idea will always outlive a bad one."

America is a good idea.

So are the ideas I've found in the Bible: freedom, oneness, compassion, gratitude, and charity, to name a few.

It's not surprising that many of the ideas that Americans value most have roots in the Bible. The founding fathers received much of their inspiration from the Old and New Testaments. America is based on the idea that we are created in the image of God:

> *We hold these truths to be self-evident, that all men are created*
> *equal, that they are endowed by their Creator with certain*
> *unalienable rights, that among these are life, liberty and the pursuit*
> *of happiness.*
> *—The Declaration of Independence*

The United States, at root, is a spiritual idea that recognizes our relationship to God and to each other. Our country is only two hundred years old, and far from living up to its highest ideals, but what a beautiful beginning!

Jesus Christ and his teachings have been important to me since I was a child. As an adult I was surprised to hear their echo in our nation's founding documents: God created us not only to know, love, and serve Him in this world and love our neighbors as ourselves but *to love and care for others in community.* The pursuit of happiness is a team sport.

Most Americans know that. That's why we get outraged at scandals like Enron, are glad to pay taxes for the good of the whole, and want to help those whose needs are greater than our own. Religion finds fertile soil here. Somehow we know: we *are* our brother's keeper, our neighbor is part of us, and what happens to the least of us, happens to all of us.

> *If one part of the body suffers, all of the other parts suffer with it;*
> *if one part benefits, all the other parts share in its joy.*
> *—1 Corinthians 12:26*

St. Paul and the founding fathers both knew: We are one body with many parts. All of them are equally important. Each one depends upon the other.

And all depend upon a Power that is larger than the whole. America is an idea, and ideas don't get much better than that.

When I was a child going to Catholic school, after a prayer we placed our hands on our hearts and pledged allegiance to the flag and to the Republic for which it stands,

*One nation under God,*
*Indivisible,*
*With liberty and justice for all.*

The Christian idea and the America idea are not the same, but the same spirit runs through them like blood through a body. Judge Learned Hand in a famous speech on I Am an American Day, 1944, said:

*The spirit of liberty remembers that not even a sparrow falls to*
*earth unheeded. The spirit of liberty is the spirit of Him whom,*
*near two thousand years ago, taught mankind that lesson it has*
*never learned, but has never quite forgotten; that there may be a*
*kingdom where the least shall be heard and considered side by side*
*with the greatest.*

And that's why I have hope for this country that I love. It is founded on a good idea. And good ideas always outlive bad ones.

As an American I'd like to think that someday the world will embrace this idea, but I know that first we must better realize it at home. We need to *become* the values we cherish most. As a Christian I am learning that we can't really change the world, but we can change the way we see ourselves and our brothers and sisters in the world. And that can make all the difference.

As an American I hope someday our friends in Europe will look at us and say, "Look at how the Americans love and care for one another!" We do, but we can do better.

As a Christian I hope that someday our brothers and sisters in Africa, Asia, and South America will look at us and say, "Look at how the Americans love and care for the world!" We do care, but we can do much better.

As an American Christian I dare to hope that someday there will not even be an America or a world. Only the perfect realization of the perfect idea,

*One body in God,*
*Indivisible,*
*With love, peace, assurance, and gratitude for all.*

After all, good ideas not only outlive bad ones but also have the potential to get better all the time.

I don't think I'll be around to see it, but as an American Christian I *know*: It's only a matter of time.

And who knows? Like the Berlin Wall, it could all begin to happen "in the twinkling of an eye. . . ."

*You may say I'm a dreamer,*
*but I'm not the only one.*
*I hope some day you'll join us,*
*and the world will live as one.*

—John Lennon, "Imagine"

I am proud to be an American Buddhist. I was raised Roman Catholic in an Italian American family, but as a young adult I found fulfillment and a feeling of peace in the Dharma. My practice lends a deeper meaning to everyday events and helps to cultivate a sense of wonder.

Not long ago being a Caucasian American practicing Buddhism was a rarity, almost a fringe culture. Today most people react to my practice with benign curiosity—even leading one friend to ask me to write a paragraph for a book called *I Like Being American*!

I enjoy the ability to live my life according to my practice. Buddhism—Soto Zen in my case—encourages individuals to experience the world directly and without illusion or mental modification. My career, where I live, and political positions are mine to consciously choose. Not all practitioners in the world have these options. Some, like Tibetan Buddhists, are openly persecuted.

As a community, Buddhists contribute to many aspects of American culture and help to encourage nonviolent conflict resolution, human rights, and advocate for sustainable environmental practices. This practice is a wonderful complement to a country that encourages personal freedoms and responsibilities.

I am thankful that our country gives me the freedom to explore my own spiritual path.

—Dominic G. Profaci
Hastings, New York

When that brilliance suffuses objects, it penetrates from the outside to the inside; when that brilliance suffuses the mind, it puts an end to ignorance.

—Buddhism

I'm proud to be an American Hindu. My great, great grandparents came from India to the island of my birth, Trinidad. They were slaves who toiled in the sugar cane fields. I'm grateful for where I came from and for the opportunity in America to give more to my children than my parents were able to give me. To my delight many other Hindus live here and instill in their children a pride in their country and a love for their faith. Hinduism is unique among the great religions of the world. It has no founder or messiah or single sacred book. We believe our religion is without beginning, and without end. As a Hindu, and as an American, I am a man of my word. I value honor. I trust my faith to keep my family and me well. What is the point of living if you don't have faith?

—Bobby Soogrim
Greenwich, Connecticut

*Those who see all creatures within themselves*
*And themselves in all creatures know no fear.*
*Those who see all creatures in themselves*
*And themselves in all creatures know no grief.*
*How can the multiplicity of life*
*Delude the one who sees its unity?*

—Hinduism

*Sane and insane, all are searching lovelorn*
*For Him, in mosque, temple, church, alike.*
*For only God is the One God of Love,*
*And Love calls from all these, each one*
*His home.*

—Sufism

God is love, and whoever lives in love, lives in God, and God in them.

—Christianity

The fabulous country—the place where miracles not only happen, but where they happen all the time.

—Thomas Wolfe, American novelist

I like the Americans because they are healthy and optimistic.

—Franz Kafka, European novelist

America is a vast conspiracy to make you happy.

—John Updike, American novelist

Most Americans are born drunk. . . . They have a sort of permanent intoxication from within, a sort of invisible champagne. . . . Americans do not need to drink to inspire them to do anything.

—G. K. Chesterton, British novelist

As I fell asleep, I thought to myself: "Well, now, I have lived one whole day in America and—just like they say—America is a country where anything, anything at all can happen. And in twenty years—about this—I never changed my mind."

—George Papashvily, Russian immigrant
*Anything Can Happen,* 1943

America is a "happy ending" nation.

—Dore Schary, American playright

The happy ending is our national belief.

—Mary McCarthy, American novelist

# Chapter Six

# AMERICAN SYMBOLS

The woman with the shining torch who welcomes newcomers to our land represents an ancient goddess who "lights the way." The book she clutches to her breast represents the Declaration of Independence. She reminds us of who we are and what we are to be:

*"Keep, ancient lands, your storied pomp!" cries she*
*With silent lips. "Give me your tired, your poor,*
*Your huddled masses yearning to be free,*
*The wretched refuse of your teeming shore.*
*Send these, the homeless, tempest-tost to me*
*I lift my lamp beside the golden door!"*

> —Emma Lazarus, American poet
> "The New Colossus"

In 1911, at the age of sixteen, Rose La Noce came to the United States from Nicosia, a small town in the hills of central Sicily. After she disembarked from the *Carpathia* at Ellis Island, immigration officials detained her. She had cried so frequently during the long voyage that the officials, noticing her red-rimmed eyes, suspected disease. Finally approved to enter the country, Rose made her way from New York City to Philadelphia, where she would board with an aunt and begin her life as a seamstress. In a few years she married a man named Thomas Spano, who came from a Sicilian town not far from her own. Together they raised three children in Philadelphia—sending a son to war and a daughter to college. And every Memorial Day, every Flag Day, every Fourth of July, and every Veteran's Day, Rose was the first on her block to push the spindly poles of her dime-store American flags deep into the earth in front of her home.

I love America because it welcomed my grandmother. And I love America for all the Roses that it continues to welcome.

—James Martin, S.J.
New York, New York

Whenever I look at the Statue of Liberty I think of my grandmother and shed a tear of gratitude.

In the late 1800s my great uncles escaped the pogroms in Poland and fled to America. They sent money back home so that my grandmother who was thirteen and her younger sister could join them. Even though my grandmother felt like she was abandoning her roots, she had the courage and foresight to come to a new land.

As an illiterate Jewish woman who never had the same opportunities as the men in her family, my grandmother never became successful in the eyes of the world. In my eyes, however, *bubha* was a strong, loving, and caring woman who made sure that I had a beautiful winter coat each year and who healed my relationship with my father whom my mother had divorced when I was five. She knew what it was like to feel abandoned and she did not want me to go through what she had experienced.

My grandfather had fled Austria in search of a better life and met my grandmother

Photo of the Statue of Liberty liberty bond

in New York. He worked hard as a pushcart salesman, selling pillows and blankets on the cobblestone streets of the Lower East Side. He also was illiterate and never became a successful businessman. But again I remember him as a kind and gentle man who, before going to work, climbed the six stories of our tenement to prepare breakfast for my brother and me.

These people were "poor Jews," but their love for their children and grandchildren was uppermost in their minds and hearts. They came to the new land so that at least their descendants could have a better life than they could ever imagine.

I am always aware of how blessed I am to be here, thanks to these brave men and women who knew when it was time to leave their countries and come to an America that welcomed them into her arms.

May the symbol of Lady Liberty forever welcome its hungry and its poor into this blessed land of grace and opportunity!

—Diane Kerievsky
Great Neck, New York

## The Flag on the Moon
BY HARRISON H. SCHMITT

Thirty years ago, I walked on the moon. Our *Apollo 17* mission in December 1972 was the last journey by humans to the moon, giving me the distinction of being the last of twelve people to step on the lunar surface. Surely I'll lose that honor someday when Americans return to live and work on our nearest celestial neighbor as its energy resources become increasingly important to life on earth. But an historic era in human exploration ended with *Apollo 17*.

The Apollo missions, like few other events in our nation's history, united this country in a common moment of joy and accomplishment. When Neil Armstrong took those first steps on the moon, every American felt a sense of pride that remains unique in our national experience. Indeed, much of humanity joined in that sense of pride.

Every crew that landed on the moon planted the American flag on the lunar surface. As the entire world watched, this colorful, vivid, and moving symbol of America and liberty was unfurled against the stark lunar landscape.

Pictures of the flag against the blackness of space or reflected in an astronaut's visor remain among the most compelling and historic images of this exciting time.

For Americans, taking the flag to the moon was the right and natural thing to do. Nothing but the flag could express so simply and so powerfully that the nation that had met President Kennedy's charge and sent its sons to explore another world. Every American—regardless of race, creed, religion, ethnic background, or political affiliation—could look at the flag and see a bit of themselves on that faraway surface. As it has in war, as it does in foreign countries, as it does each and every day in schools and stadiums and federal buildings, the flag on the moon stood for each of us—and for all of us. It symbolized the power of free men and women when they reach to meet a challenge.

Americans treasure their flag because we, as a nation, treasure the values and history for which it stands, the values that form a common thread uniting a diverse society. Americans treasure the patriotism, the honor, and the sense of common purpose embodied in our flag. And as we hold those values to be sacred, we hold sacred the flag that stands as their most visible symbol.

**Harrison H. Schmitt**, a geologist, was an astronaut from 1965 to 1975, and served as a United States Senator from New Mexico from 1977 to 1983.

A single fabric of lovely colors and multiple threads. AMY-BETH PITURA

He is currently an adjunct professor at the University of Wisconsin College of Engineering.

Having learned to stand by the flag, may we also learn to stand by what the flag symbolizes; to stand up for equal rights, universal freedom, for justice to all, for a true republic.

—James F. Clarke, American minister

To me the flag has been more than merely an inspiration. Ever since my first game in Eau Claire in the Northern League in 1952, I have been aiming at the flag, in more ways than one.

—Hank Aaron

American home run champion

*Hushed the people's swelling murmur,*
*Whilst the boy cries joyously;*
*"Ring!" he's shouting, "ring, grandfather,*
*Ring! Oh, ring for Liberty!"*
*Quickly at the given signal*
*The old bellman lifts his hand. Iron music through the land.*

—G. S. Hillard, *Franklin Fifth Reader*

## Mending the Liberty Bell
### BY LEONARD FEIN

My fist has never connected with human flesh. (Ah, but how many walls?) Still, I wanted to haul off and punch him, I pussycat.

The occasion for this visceral reaction (punches commence in the viscera, I've now learned), on which I am pleased and relieved to report I did not act, was a panel discussion in which I recently participated. I'd said in passing, in response to a question from the audience, that "I love this country." The panelist who followed me, an American who made *aliya* some years back, turned to me and said, "I don't believe you meant to say 'love.' How can you love America, given the way it's treated its Jews?"

The way it's treated its Jews? Perhaps I might have understood if he'd said, "the way it's treated its Indians" or "the way it treats its people of color" or "the way it worships golden calves." But the way it's treated its Jews?

The truth, however, is that I was less interested in persuading my interlocutor than in repairing whatever damage he might have done to the audience, which was composed of Jewish college students from around the country. So, when a day later I had another go at them, I told them a story that was among my late father's favorites, a story he told the night he was honored for his years of service as a professor at the Baltimore Hebrew College:

When I was a boy, the *rebbe* in our *cheder* in Benderi [Bessarabia] said to us one day, "Children, they say that very far away there is a country called America, and I suppose that is so, for why would they lie about such a thing? And they say as well that in that faraway country called America, there is a city called Philadelphia, and I suppose that too is so. And they go on to say that in the city called Philadelphia, there is a bell they call the Liberty Bell and that on that bell are proclaimed the words from our book: 'Proclaim liberty throughout the land and to all the inhabitants thereof.' Frankly, I find that hard to believe. Why would they write our words on their bell?

"I have a favor to ask you now. If it should happen when you grow up that you go to America, try to visit the place they call Philadelphia and see the bell. And write and tell me whether it is true that they have inscribed our words on their bell. I would like to know such a thing."

My father continued,

As it happened, I did come to America, and I chanced to Philadelphia, and I went to see the bell, and yes, indeed, there were the words, our words. But the bell was cracked.

You honor me tonight for my life as a teacher. I prefer to think of myself as a person who has sought to be a bell-mender.

To the young people in front of me, I added one line to my father's story: "The bell is still cracked."

And to my interlocutor of the preceding day, in our quick post-session minute, I said, "How can one not love a country that leaves so much room to its bell-menders, among whom so many Jews choose to be counted?"

To say nothing, of course, of how this country has treated and treats its Jews. (Were I to say something about that, what I'd say is simply, "Look around.")

**Leonard Fein** is the founder of Americans for Peace Now, an author, and a columnist for the *Forward* newspaper.

The yearning to make life tolerable is best revealed, it seems to me, in the American smile. You meet on American streets smiling faces, which plunge you into a stream of quite general and anonymous good feeling. . . .

I remember I was in Washington on a day in 1940, when the first news arrived of the invasion of France by the Germans. I was in utter loneliness, with personal problems and anxieties that weighed heavily on me. In this frame of mind I went to a small restaurant to have lunch, and was served by a waitress who displayed for me a sweet anonymous American smile. I knew perfectly well that it was mere illusion, as unreal a thing as "the smile of an absent cat." And nevertheless I felt comforted by this mirage, all the more comforted as I knew I had absolutely nothing to expect from these merely symbolic good feelings, and therefore no possibility of being disappointed.

And I suddenly realized the meaning of this symbol, the general, elementary, deep-seated sense of common human pilgrimage and brotherhood which exists in this country and lies behind the smile in question. After all, to feel disheartened and forsaken was only an episode. I am grateful to this waitress for having helped me one day against hopelessness.

Deep beneath the anonymous American smile there is a feeling that is evangelical in origin, compassion for man, a desire to make life tolerable. This symbolic smile is a kind of anonymous reply of the human soul, which refuses to acknowledge itself vanquished by the pressure of the assembly line, or the big anonymous machinery of modern civilization.

—Jacques Maritain
French philosopher
*The Symbolic Smile*

## Little Shrines at Firehouses, and Other Symbol Experiences

BY KATHY COFFEY

I began with a bias. As a girl traveling through Europe with my parents, I noticed two distinct styles of relating to other countries. My mother would delight in German rieslings, French impressionists, and Swiss Alps. While appreciating the textures, colors and tastes of other countries, my father would gradually lean into his pro-U.S. stance.

"Ah, it won't be long now," he'd whisper over cold British toast or raw German hamburger. "I'm gonna walk onto that plane, and that nice American girl will be standing there in her airline uniform. She will say 'hello' in English and smile, and I will kiss her on both cheeks."

Part of me always wondered if he'd really do it, this distinguished, introverted professor, not given to displays of affection. But after six weeks or so away from home, I was ready to kiss her too. She represented the WELCOME HOME banner of the familiar, the beacon of all that was intimate and dear. She was a smiling symbol, one who stood for baseball and peanut butter sandwiches, Election Day, Disneyland, Thanksgiving, the Golden Gate, and guaranteed freedoms.

There is a certain wisdom in the idea that God has us exactly where God wants us, popularized as the saying "bloom where you are planted." As I look at where I've been planted, I see that it's good ground, beautiful ground, sacred ground.

One blessing of my current career as a writer and speaker has been travel throughout the United States. The airport, despite problems, represents for me the portal to adventure. I like seeing the whole country: the jade waters off the Florida Keys, the surf crashing along the Oregon coast, the blue haze over the Smokies, Chicago's Navy Pier, the gardens of North Carolina, Minnesota's lakes, the historic mansions of New Orleans, the towering peaks of the Tetons. Whenever I cross the Potomac River into Washington, D.C., seeing the panorama of monuments and Tidal Basin, my throat tightens with emotion.

I also like meeting the wide variety of people: the crusty easterner with the heart of a marshmallow, the refined Asian American of San Francisco, the earthy humor of an African American in Houston, the gracious ease of a New Mexican artist. When they have hospitably welcomed me, they have proudly shared their locale, their roots in bayou, forest, or plain, their customs, music, and unique accents. We may criticize the government and work for change, but I suspect we all get misty-eyed when our national anthem plays at the Olympics.

We Americans cherish the right to dissent, at the same time knowing that people are so desperate to live here, they risk their lives to cross the border. Because we descended from rebels, our peculiarly American pantheon reveres nonconformist heroes: Jane Addams, Chief Seattle, Thoreau, Susan B. Anthony, Harriet Tubman, Governor Ralph Carr (who refused to inter Japanese Americans during World War II), Dorothy Day, Cesar Chavez, Martin Luther King, Jr., Fannie Lou Hamer, Flannery O'Connor, Jean Donovan.

Even prison inmates appreciate American freedoms. Women trapped in a punitive system that separates them from their children for years complain angrily. But they also defend their rights stoutly. "No matter how bad it gets," says a self-described drug addict and thief, "I know they can't drag me out in the middle of the night and shoot me." Our penal system may be convoluted and sometimes unjust, but we are shocked when we read that killing political prisoners is the primary way the Chinese harvest organs for donation. We are stunned by systems where the penalty for theft is the loss of a hand.

While September 11, 2001, was for many a wake-up call to how some people hate us, others found in the sobering events of that day an affirmation of the best that is American. The language of symbol was eloquent after the tragedy: flags of all nations hanging at half-mast along Washington's Embassy Row, little shrines at firehouses, the Olympic torch borne by survivors, the tattered flag carried into the opening of the Salt Lake City Games.

Perhaps symbol is the best language in which to speak of love for one's country. Words quickly become inflated and jingoistic. They are too narrow a vehicle to contain the depth of emotion. For that, we must rely on the sight of a torch held aloft by a statue in a harbor, an obelisk piercing the sky in memory of the founder, an eternal flame guarding the tomb of an unknown soldier, an empty cell at the Birmingham jail, and the sound of music drifting over the Atlantic, the Appalachians, the Great Lakes, the Rockies, the Pacific:

*Oh beautiful for spacious skies, for amber waves of grain, for purple mountains' majesty above the fruited plain . . .*

**Kathy Coffey** of Denver, Colorado, is the author of several books on spirituality, including *God in the Moment,* and an editor at Living the Good News Press.

I love the symbols of being a SAM (Suburban American Mom): decorating the kids' bikes for the local Memorial Day parade; the oohs and aahs at the Fourth of July fireworks with family and friends; the flags waving at schools, post office, village hall, and so many homes. SAMs nurture and pump life—their talents and hopes—to the rest of the country via the arteries of station wagons, commuter trains, and big yellow school buses. They are as American as apple pie. Like mothers in cities and in rural areas, they spend their lives selecting and gathering the best apples of family values, religion, education, and service. They add the cinnamon spice of sports, scouts, and citizenship. All the while they keep a vigilant eye on the errant unwanted seeds of violence, addiction, and hatred. I am grateful that I was a SAM in the years when life seemed less insane. I've advanced to Suburban American Grandma (SAG) now, and am grateful for this new experience!

—Paula Dore
Glenview, Illinois

I like America because we can put on our nickels "In God We Trust." I like America because in Washington, D.C., we have dwellings for a president, Supreme Court justices, Congress—we have a democracy. I

like America because of Thanksgiving Day, July 4th, Memorial Day—
we have a rich heritage. I like America because it is home, a place that
has nurtured me and called me to freedom and responsibility.

—Bishop Robert Morneau
Green Bay, Wisconsin

Hank Miller's symbolic photograph *I Am the Wall.*
"Touch me. Don't be afraid. I can't hurt you. . . ."

## Touch Me—A Soliloquy

BY HANK MILLER

*Touch me. Don't be afraid. I can't hurt you.*
*Go ahead and touch my smooth surface.*
*Feel the cold, glasslike smoothness and the*
*crevices and lines that make me what I am.*
*Use both hands if you wish. We are more*
*similar than you dare to believe.*

*Touch my face. Yes, I have a face like yours.
It has weathered the centuries as yours has
the years. My face portrays my evolution.
Yours, the birth and death of a generation.
My face has aged like yours as we have
endured together the testimony of earth's
elements.*

*I have eyes like yours. My inscriptions stare
out at you as I search for the meaning of
why we are here. I look into your eyes and
see who you are. Who am I? I was formed
millions of years past and now you see the
results of my evolution.*

*I can feel your hands and the sweat from
your palms flows into the countless
combination of the letters that make me. I
know you. I have known you since I was able
to breathe in the air as my smoothness
began to take shape and my color matured
along with natural flaws. You have known
me since the days when you came to take me
from my mother.*

*You cannot hear me. I am static and
unmoving. But I can hear your murmurs
and your cries of pain and sadness. Your
sons and daughters ask why? There are no
answers.*

*I am very old. I have seen everything, and I
am none the wiser for the pain and suffering
I have witnessed since I rose from the bowels
of the earth. I have witnessed the conflict,
the death, the civilizations, and the societies*

*that have come before you. Yet I remain*
*mystified about this day.*

*I feel sad yet alive with a purpose. I have*
*come to know those who are now an integral*
*part of the reason for my being here at this*
*place and time. That purpose has become*
*apparent as I stand before you on this day*
*while your brethren gather to witness my*
*reflections and the changes of light that*
*mirror your soul.*

*I am a reflection of you. . . .*

*I am all of you. . . .*

*I am your spirit. . . .*

*I am the Wall.*

**Hank Miller** of Mill Valley, California, is a freelance writer, former Navy pilot, and a Vietnam veteran whose comrades' names are inscribed on the Wall. For further information please contact lckt13@earthlink.net.

When I was pregnant with our first child, my husband got the call for his draft physical. Next stop, Vietnam. Tom was a teacher at the time, and his administrator spoke to the draft board about the need to allow him to continue to teach. The draft board classified Tom 4F, exempt from active duty.

We were so thankful that we vowed to spend the rest of our lives not only observing our national holidays of Memorial Day and the Fourth of July but also participating in them with all our hearts. To this day we view those holidays as a time to thank God for the men and women who have sacrificed their lives for the freedoms that we must never take for granted. We lost friends in the Vietnam War, so these holidays are personal.

Our little community has the oldest Memorial Day observation in the State of Wisconsin. Tom and I built a floral float that is lowered into the river during the playing of Taps. Watching the float glide down the river reminds the community of the cost of our precious freedoms. So many have given their lives so that we can live in peace, assurance, and, yes, gratitude.

—Sue Johnson
Waterford, Wisconsin

The eagle, full of the boundless spirit of freedom, living above the valleys, strong and powerful in his might, has become the national emblem of a country that offers freedom in word and thought and an opportunity for a full and free expansion into the boundless space of the future.

—Maude M. Grant, baldeagleinfo.com

I wish that the bald eagle had not been chosen as the representative of our country, he is a bird of bad moral character, he does not get his living honestly, you may have seen him perched on some dead tree, where, too lazy to fish for himself, he watches the labor of the fishing-hawk, and when that diligent bird has at length taken a fish, and is bearing it to its nest for the support of his mate and young ones, the bald eagle pursues him and takes it from him. . . . Besides he is a rank coward; the little kingbird, not bigger than a sparrow attacks him boldly and drives him out of the district. He is therefore by no means a proper emblem for the brave and honest . . . of America. . . . For a truth, the turkey is in comparison a much more respectable bird, and withal a true original native of America . . . a bird of courage, and would not hesitate to attack a grenadier of the British guards, who should presume to invade his farmyard with a red coat on.

—Benjamin Franklin
American statesman

Ground Zero: a holy place. PHOTO BY NIKO

The eagle is an ancient symbol of spiritual vision. It was supposed to be the only creature that could look directly into the sun. . . . The olive branch in the eagle's dexter talon symbolizes peace. Its presence there is a radical departure from the heraldry of the Old World. The eagles of the monarchies which preceded the United States usually carried the symbols of war on the dexter side. Our national arms proclaim the principle that the primary aim of the United States shall be to establish peace. Hence the eagle faces the olive branch.

—Paul Foster Case
American Freemason
*Builders of the Adytum*

This place [Ground Zero] has to be sanctified. It has to become a place, when anybody comes, that they immediately feel the power, strength, and emotion of what it means to become an American. . . .

Long after we are all gone, it's the sacrifice of our patriots and their heroism that this place is going to be remembered for. This is going to be a place that is remembered 100 and 1,000 years from now, like the great battlefields of Europe and of the United States. And we really have to be able to do with it what they did with Normandy or Valley Forge or Bunker Hill or Gettysburg. We have to be able to create something here that enshrines this forever and that allows people to build on it and grow from it.

—Rudy Giuliani, former Mayor of
New York City

Why do I like being American? In America baseball is the national pastime. Where else could I find that?

—Yogi Berra, American Yankee

Let's play two!

—Ernie Banks, American Cub

Say, hey!

—Willie Mays, American Giant

Baseball is a public trust. Players turn over, owners turn over, and certain commissioners turn over. But baseball goes on.

—Peter Ueberroth, former head of the U.S. Olympic Committee and Commissioner of Major League Baseball

Merit will win. It was promised by baseball.

—A. Bartlett Giamatti, former President of Yale University and Commissioner of Major League Baseball

Don't look back. Something might be gaining on you.

—Satchel Paige, American legend

# Chapter Seven

# THE AMERICAN HERO

I think of a hero as someone who understands the degree of responsibility that comes with his freedom.

> —Bob Dylan, American songwriter

Heroism is not just pulling a child from a burning house or a driver from an icy river or a kitten from a tall tree. Heroism is also holding the door for a frail elderly person and driving courteously and cooperatively and listening with an attentive heart to a friend's words. Small daily acts of love are as heroic as big, once-in-a-lifetime acts of rescue.

> —L. M. Heroux, American writer

True heroism is remarkably sober, very undramatic. It is not the urge to surpass all others at whatever cost, but the urge to serve others at whatever cost.

> —Arthur Ashe
> American tennis champion

When the first *Superman* movie came out I was frequently asked, "What is a hero?" My answer was that a hero is someone who commits a courageous action without considering the consequences. . . . Now my definition is completely different. I think a hero is an ordinary individual who finds strength to persevere and endure in spite of overwhelming obstacles.

> —Christopher Reeve, American actor

## Five American Role Models
### BY MICHAEL LEACH

"I'm not a role model," declared Charles Barkley a few years ago. The basketball star struck a nerve and pointed to a truth. "Just because I can play basketball," he said, "doesn't mean I can raise your kids."

When contemporary athletes turn down the job of role model (or fall short) we return to the pedestals of our past: Abraham Lincoln, Babe Ruth, Amelia Earhart, Rosa Parks, and the like. We overlook the living role models who are in front of our eyes—who stand tall on their own and lead and support us every day of their lives. They are ordinary people who persevere in heroic, everyday acts of patience, kindness, dedication, and service. They are (among others) our parents, teachers, volunteers, firefighters, and, for want of a better word, our G.I.'s.

It is time to make pedestals for five new American role models.

1. *The American parent.* From the soccer mom in Seattle who juggles a vocation as homemaker with a job at Microsoft to the single mom in Chicago who has to work two jobs but always makes breakfast for her kids and always prays with them at bedtime, the American Mom is a hero. From the dad in Atlanta whose work takes him across the country but who has never missed a little league game or a recital to the father of five in Fargo who changes diapers, does the wash, and balances the checkbook, the American Dad is a hero. Sure, *some* moms and dads don't deserve the title, but we're celebrating the best of them here, and that's the majority of them. Thank you, American parent!

2. *The American teacher.* Three million men and women teach 54 million American children in 118,000 public and private schools, K through 12. In addition, 930,000 full- and part-time teachers prepare 15 million students in 4,000 colleges and universities nationwide. Ask any athlete or actor or tycoon who influenced them most and chances are they'll say, first their parents, and second a teacher who believed in them. Ask yourself. Thank you, American teacher!

3. *The American volunteer.* More than 110 million American adults volunteer 20 billion hours a year helping their neighbors through civic, religious, and other private organizations. Sixty-two percent of American women and 49

percent of American men volunteer an average of 3.5 hours a week. From the grandmother who gives you sweets after you donate blood to the teenager who hands out food to famine victims overseas, American volunteers are the heart of our country. Thank you, American volunteer!

4. *The American firefighter.* It took September 11th to remind us of what we take for granted: the men and women who risk their lives saving the lives of others. We will always remember the photo of our firefighters raising the flag on the rubble of Ground Zero just as we revere the image of our marines planting the flag on Iwo Jima. We will never forget their heroism, nor that of the police and paramedics and emergency workers, and we vow to keep in mind that these men and women perform heroic acts of simple kindness every single day. Thank you, American firefighter, and all your brothers and sisters!

5. *The American G.I.* Few people stand taller in our history than the men who crawled through the mud at Normandy, who patrol the skies and live in boats at the bottom of the sea to protect us, who are ambassadors of good-will on every continent for the sake of peace. One does not have to be political to appreciate the men and women who serve in our army, navy, air force, and marines. No one knows better than they that there's got to be a better way. Until that day, thank you, American G.I.!

Ralph Waldo Emerson, the American philosopher, wrote: "A hero is no braver than an ordinary man, but he is braver five minutes longer." Parents, teachers, volunteers, firefighters, and G.I.'s are ordinary people who persevere and finish the race without benefit of fame or fortune. They are our new American role models.

*In 1993, Robert De Niro directed and starred in* A Bronx Tale, *a movie about a devoted father (Lorenzo) who drives a bus and whose son (Calogero) hero-worships a local mob boss (Sonny)—but only for a while. The following is a snippet of dialogue from this wonderful movie:*

> *Calogero:* Sonny was right. The working man is a sucker. He's a sucker.
> *Lorenzo:* He's wrong. It doesn't take much strength to pull a trigger.

But try getting up for work day after day making a living. Let's see him try that. Then we'll see who's the real tough guy. The working man's the tough guy. Your father's the tough guy.

*Calogero:* But everyone loves him.

*Lorenzo:* They don't love him. They fear him. That's the difference.

## My American Mom
### BY SASHA STONE

Imagine being confined to an institution surrounded by a ten-foot iron fence with a locked gate and soldiers with big guns guarding it. You have never been outside the gates so you know nothing of the world. You have no family, no one to love you or care about you, very little food to eat, ragged clothing and shoes that don't fit. You are spanked with a carpet whipper, have your tongue snipped by scissors because you want to talk when it is time to sleep.

The people hired to watch after you give you vodka to make you be quiet and stand you in a corner with a urine-drenched sheet wrapped around your head and have other children laugh at you because you wet the bed. They only laugh because they are afraid of what will happen to them if they don't.

You are called many ugly names but don't know what your real name is. You don't know how old you are and have never celebrated a birthday. You are told that you were left because you were bad and if you learn to behave yourself, your parents might come to get you someday. You watch children being burned with cigarettes and having their hands pressed onto hot lightbulbs be-

"I knew she was going to take care of me and that everything would be all right."

cause they rock their heads to go to sleep. You have never heard of God or had anything that you could call yours.

Until I was six and a half years old, I lived in an orphanage in Siberia. This was my life. I was robbed of my identity, robbed of being a child, robbed of having a family, robbed of having a mother to love and hold me, and robbed of the freedom to know God. The caretakers would look in a different direction or walk away when they saw one of the other workers hurting children. It was like see no evil, hear no evil, say no evil. Nobody cared what happened. I just wanted to die because I felt so beaten down.

Then one day there was a Good Samaritan who came on a long journey from the other side of the world. When she came upon me, she felt compassion and love. She hugged me and kissed me and wanted to heal all my wounds. Although she didn't know my language and I didn't know her language and our countries' beliefs were very different, I knew she was going to take care of me and that everything was going to be all right.

We both felt afraid, and she was unsure about just how she was going to get me out of there. She was convinced God had not directed her halfway around the world to leave me. When I was afraid to sleep at night because I thought I would wet the bed and she wouldn't like me, she would hold me tight in her lap and rock me to sleep. She called me by my name, Sasha, and told me how old I was. She gave me food and brought me new clothes that were nice and warm and mine. She gave me shoes that were for a boy and that fit my feet. She loved everything about me. All the things I had been punished for were the things she said made me so special. She told me how sorry she was that I hadn't been her baby and promised me she would be my mother forever and I would never have to be alone again.

My Good Samaritan brought me to America, where I had a sister waiting for me. She taught me about God. She sent me to Catholic school so I could hear about Jesus every day. On the first birthday I celebrated in my new family and new country, I had seven parties to make up for all the birthdays I never got to celebrate.

My Good Samaritan has taught me love and compassion. She has taught me never to look the other way when there is someone in need. She has taught me to be like Christ and to recognize our neighbor as the next hurting person we meet, friend or not. God reached out to me with his love and mercy in my hurting world. Since then our family has adopted three more children.

Although my mom reminds me that we are not a materially rich family, our "inheritance" is secure and our hearts are filled with love, mercy, and power.

**Sasha Stone**, an eighth-grader at St. Jane de Chantal School in Bethesda, Maryland, won the 2002 Francis X. Ford Award, named after a Maryknoll missioner who died in a communist prison in 1952, for this loving tribute to his American mom.

I had to write a paragraph in third grade called "My Hero." I chose my dad. He was a World War II hero, and my hero. I wrote that paragraph more than fifty years ago. Dad passed away three weeks ago. And now I'm at home working on a chapter in this book called "The American Hero." My dad—Glen Leach—is still my hero and always will be. A loving father, a teacher of kindness, a man who gave to others without expecting anything in return, and, yes, a World War II hero as real as any in *Saving Private Ryan*. In short, he reflected just about everything I wrote about in "Five American Role Models." I'm grateful to have this opportunity to show you what he looked like.

—Michael Leach

I feel blessed to be an elementary public school teacher, and to share the enthusiasm of my colleagues for our vocation. Our school has a high percentage of children and families who are new to America. Our profession challenges us to model and instill the core values that make our country strong. Our curriculum strives for excellence in not only academics but citizenship as well. Values such as hard work, fairness, responsibility, mutual respect, and appreciation for our differences are more than words. They are living ideas that express our nation's soul, and to sow these seeds in the minds and hearts of our children is to benefit them for life. I am proud that as an American I can achieve my own goals if I follow these lessons. I am equally proud to teach them to my students.

—Chris Leach

P.S. 25, Bronx, New York

It took the events of 9/11 to awaken the public to some of America's unsung heroes. But teachers, unlike the military and civil uniformed members of society, rarely have opportunities to display courage through acts of valor. They are not risk takers, but steady, hard-working, compassionate people who daily plug away at an unglamorous but important job. Yet, when high-profile leaders of any society are asked about their accomplishments, they inevitably point to a teacher who inspired them. Teachers do not need medals or ticker tape parades. Their reward is the unwavering faith that they have forwarded the culture of mankind. I believe that is an act of heroism.

—Dominic Butera, Principal, Cos Cob

Elementary School, Connecticut

The generosity of Americans is truly something to behold. Did you know that more than 56 percent of the people of the United States are currently volunteering some amount of time in the course of a year, giving an estimated 19.9 billion hours? It's the highest rate of participation of any industrialized nation.

The majority volunteer on a regular basis. And thousands more serve as full-time volunteers—whether for a summer, a year, or as their life's work.

Intrepid, they reject the notion that things are not possible to change. They know that to achieve progress, voluntary citizen action must be applied through an organized framework. We at the Commission on Voluntary Service and Action (CVSA) describe this process as ordinary people achieving extraordinary things. For truly we have, and we do.

Today the average working American labors ten to thirteen hours a day, with many of the lowest-paid working ninety hours or more a week, often at multiple jobs and with diminishing pay. Some 45 million people in the United States have no health insurance; 35 million more are underinsured. With growing constraints on their time, many look to participate not in charities, handouts, or government-funded programs, but in independent volunteer efforts. The more challenging things get, the more Americans volunteer.

It's a good thing they do. Worldwide, 800-plus million people are hungry right now. One in five of the world's people—1.2 billion—live on less than a dollar a day. The people in more than fifty countries have lower real per capita incomes today than they did a decade ago. As Americans, we have tremendous resources and resourcefulness within our reach. As volunteers, we have an unprecedented opportunity to advance not only the people of this country, but also those in other countries who presently suffer unimaginable privation.

We own a volunteer tradition stretching back to the citizens' committees of the American struggle for independence. Thousands of independent grassroots organizations, large and small, are growing and struggling, working for dignity and decency for all people throughout this nation and the world.

As a full-time volunteer working in America with these organizations and the people who build them, and with an understanding of the conditions prevailing in the world as a whole—I wouldn't be doing anything else anywhere else if you paid me!

—Susan Angus, Executive Director
Commission on Voluntary Service
and Action, New York, New York

When I first felt the call to become a volunteer, I looked for something I knew would make me happy: working with animals. Now I care for injured and orphaned wildlife as a volunteer for the Wildlife Trust. Whenever I finish an afternoon of feeding and tending creatures that would otherwise die—rabbits, possums, squirrels, owls, and songbirds—I come home elated, filled with love and appreciation for the wonders of nature. In a small way, I have been helpful.

I also volunteer at Pegasus Therapeutic Riding (horseback riding for the handicapped). Although I was drawn to it because of my experience with horses, I learned at once how blessed it is to volunteer for something that makes children happy. I feel so privileged to spend time with them that whenever we have a break in the riding program I weep at the thought of not seeing them again for a few weeks.

After the tragedy of September 11, I experienced the gratitude that comes from volunteering with others for the good of everyone. Along with hundreds of thousands of others I volunteered for the American Red Cross. Now as I help out in bloodmobiles, I see the goodness that brings Americans together, not for profit, but solely to give something back in a spirit of thanksgiving for all the gifts we too often take for granted.

—Elise Elliott
Greenwich, Connecticut

Service to others is the rent you pay for your room on earth.
—Muhammad Ali, American
boxing champion

WWW.VOLUNTEERMATCH.ORG

Feel like doing a good deed? There are plenty of ways you can help others. Just type in your ZIP code and interests (tutoring, assisting seniors, the environment, among others) and this site will direct you to your ideal Good Samaritan organization.

—A Top Ten Web site as
recommended in
www.onmagazine.com.
January/February 2002

Ask any firefighter if he can tell you who a hero is and he will tell you about someone he worked with and what they did. He will never tell you about himself. I have seen many brave acts in my seventeen years in the fire department. Some have been heroic. At the World Trade Center many firefighters continued on to the North Tower, even after the South Tower had fallen. They wrote their wills on pieces of paper on their way there in city buses and stuck them in their pockets. People needed help and that was that. Afterward families needed help and they were there. For these many months they looked for the bodies of the victims day after day. Funerals were attended on a daily basis. Keeping at it for so long is nothing short of heroic. They are in it for the long haul long after bravery has passed.

—Joe McAuley
Queens, New York

*Editor's note: Fire Marshal McAuley chose to write about his brethren in the New York City Fire Department, not himself, which is so characteristic. I can tell you that he was among those who willingly placed themselves in danger even after the first of the Twin Towers had collapsed at the World Trade Center on September 11, 2001.*

I will never look at a firefighter the same way again. What is in someone, hundreds of them, to compel them to run into a burning building while everyone else is running out, just to save people they don't even know? Their bravery has become part of our collective national legacy. Their bravery dignifies us all.

—Rev. Bill Hybels
Willow Creek Community Church
South Barrington, Illinois

Today is Veterans Day. I am a Sister of St. Joseph who serves as chaplain for our local veterans group. I watch my brother Mark, a disabled veteran from Vietnam, proudly put on his uniform. Mark has been chosen to be the flag bearer for the parade. "You look wonderful," I tell him.

At the formation area I see Pete and give him a hug. Pete's a

World War II vet and was a POW. He has a kind spirit and a gentle heart. There is Dale, carrying his oxygen tank; he was a marine in Vietnam and was sprayed with chemicals. And here is John, standing tall; he's an air force gunner from Korea, wearing his Purple Heart. Elliot arrives last, walking with a limp; he's a Vietnam vet who stepped on a land mine.

Over the past several years my admiration for these heroic men has grown, for I've come to learn that my freedom has come at great cost.

As I stand at the end of the route waiting for the parade, I notice a very old couple across the street. She stands protectively over her husband, who is hunched over on a lawn chair; he wears a Marine Corps sweatshirt and is surely a World War I vet. As my brother the flag bearer comes into view, the old man grips the arms of the chair, rises, stands straight, and offers a strong salute.

After my brother passes I hurry across the street, take the old vet's hand, and say, "Thank you!"

For me, being an American means having a deeply grateful heart.

—Mary Margaret Doorley, C.S.J.
Uniontown, Pennsylvania

## The Night Before Christmas
BY MAJOR BRUCE LOVELY, USAF

*Twas the night before Christmas, he lived all alone,*
*In a one-bedroom house made of plaster and stone.*
*I had come down the chimney with presents to give,*
*And to see who in this home did live.*

*I looked all about, a strange sight I did see,*
*No tinsel, no presents, not even a tree.*
*No stockings by mantle, just boots filled with sand,*
*On the wall hung pictures of far distant lands.*

*With medals and badges, awards of all kinds,*
*A sober thought came through my mind.*
*For this house was different, it was dark and dreary;*
*I found the home of a soldier, once I could see clearly.*

*The soldier lay sleeping, silent, alone,*
*Curled up on the floor in the one-bedroom home.*
*The face was so gentle, the room in such disorder,*
*Not how I pictured a United States soldier.*

*Was this the hero of whom I'd just read?*
*Curled up on a poncho, the floor for a bed?*
*I realized the families that I saw this night,*
*Owed their lives to these soldiers who were willing to fight.*

*Soon round the world, the children would play,*
*And grown-ups would celebrate a bright Christmas day.*
*They all enjoyed freedom, each month of the year,*
*Because of these soldiers, like the one lying here.*

*I couldn't help wonder how many lay alone,*
*On a cold Christmas eve, in a land far from home.*
*The very thought brought a tear to my eye,*
*I dropped to my knees and started to cry.*

*The soldier awakened, and I heard a rough voice,*
*Santa, don't cry, this life is my choice.*

*I fight for freedom, I don't ask for more,*
*My life is my God, my country, my corps.*
*The soldier rolled over and drifted to sleep,*
*I couldn't control it, I continued to weep.*

*I kept watch for hours, silent and still,*
*And we both shivered from the cold night's chill.*
*I didn't want to leave on that dark, cold night,*
*This guardian of honor, so willing to fight.*

*Then the soldier rolled over, with a voice soft and pure,*
*Whispered, Carry on Santa, it's Christmas day, all is secure.*
*One look at my watch and I knew he was right,*
*Merry Christmas my friend, and to all a good night.*

*"Wisht somebody would tell me there's a Santa Claus."*

**Major Lovely** wrote this poem in Korea on Christmas Eve in 1993. To honor the soldiers who were there, he put copies under their doors. Years later he saw it printed in the *Fort Leavenworth Lamp.* Today it inspires people on more than a dozen Web sites.

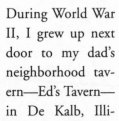

During World War II, I grew up next door to my dad's neighborhood tavern—Ed's Tavern—in De Kalb, Illinois. When the young men who were his customers went into the service, they always came back to the tavern to visit Ed, and oftentimes gave him a shoulder patch from their uniform. Ed took a picture of each serviceman, and by the end of the war, he had a banner of 175 patches, and one full wall of glass-covered black-and-white photos of local men who served to protect our freedom. I like being an American, and I'd like to thank all those brave men who helped make this a wonderful nation.

—Joan Rohlik Petitti
St. Pete Beach, Florida

*On June 14, 1999,* Time *magazine published a special issue honoring American heroes of the twentieth century. General Colin Powell wrote the following feature essay.*

## The American G.I.

### BY COLIN POWELL

As Chairman of the Joint Chiefs of Staff, I referred to the men and women of the armed forces as "G.I.s." It got me in trouble with some of my colleagues at the time. Several years earlier, the Army had officially excised the term as an unfavorable characterization derived from the designation "government issue." Sailors and Marines wanted to be known as sailors and marines. Airmen, notwithstanding their origins as a rib of the Army, wished to be called simply airmen. Collectively, they were blandly referred to as "service members."

I persisted in using G.I.s and found I was in good company. Newspapers and television shows used it all the time. The most famous and successful government education program was known as the G.I. Bill, and it still uses that title for a newer generation of veterans. When you added one of the most common boy's names to it, you got G.I. Joe, and the name of the most popular boy's toy ever, the G.I. Joe action figure. And let's not forget G.I. Jane.

G.I. is a World War II term that two generations later continues to conjure up the warmest and proudest memories of a noble war that pitted pure good against pure evil—and good triumphed. The victors in that war were the American G.I.s, the Willies and Joes, the farmer from Iowa and the steelworker from Pittsburgh who stepped off a landing craft into the hell of Omaha Beach.

The G.I. was the wisecracking kid Marine from Brooklyn who clawed his way up a deadly hill on a Pacific island. He was a black fighter pilot escorting white bomber pilots over Italy and Germany, proving that skin color had nothing to do with skill or courage. He was a native Japanese American infantryman released from his own country's concentration camp to join the fight. She was a nurse relieving the agony of a dying teenager. He was a petty officer standing on the edge of a heaving aircraft carrier with two signal paddles in his hands, helping guide a dive-bomber pilot back onto the deck.

They were America. They reflected our diverse origins. They were the embodiment of the American spirit of courage and dedication. They were truly a "people's army," going forth on a crusade to save democracy and freedom, to defeat tyrants, to save oppressed peoples, and to make their families proud of them. They were the Private Ryans, and they stood firm in the thin red line. . . .

Their forebears went by other names: doughboys, Yanks, buffalo soldiers, Johnny Reb, RoughRiders. But "G.I." will be forever lodged in the consciousness of our nation to apply to them all. The G.I. carried the value system of the American people. The G.I.s were the surest guarantee of America's commitment. For more than two hundred years, they answered the call to fight the nation's battles. They never went forth as mercenaries on the road to conquest. They went forth as reluctant warriors, as citizen soldiers.

They were as gentle in victory as they were vicious in battle. I've had survivors of Nazi concentration camps tell me of the joy they experienced as the G.I.s liberated them: America had arrived! I've had a wealthy Japanese businessman come into my office and tell me what it was like for him as a child to await the arrival of the dreaded American beasts, and instead met a smiling G.I. who gave him a Hershey bar. In thanks, the businessman was donating a large sum of money to the USO. After thanking him, I gave him as a souvenir a Hershey bar I had autographed. He took it and began to cry.

The twentieth century can be called many things, but it was most certainly a century of war. The American G.I.s helped defeat fascism and communism. They came home in triumph from the ferocious battlefields of World Wars I and II. In Korea and Vietnam they fought just as bravely as any of their predecessors, but no triumphant receptions awaited them at home. They soldiered on through the twilight struggles of the cold war and showed what they were capable of in Desert Storm. The American people took them into their hearts again.

In this century hundreds of thousands of G.I.s died to bring to the beginning of the twenty-first century the victory of democracy as the ascendant political system on the face of the earth. The G.I.s were willing to travel far away and give their lives, if necessary, to secure the rights and freedoms of others. Only a nation such as ours, based on a firm moral foundation, could make such a request of its citizens. And the G.I.s wanted nothing more than to get the job done and then return home safely. All they asked for in repayment from those they freed was the opportunity to help them become part of the world of democracy—and just enough land to bury their fallen comrades, beneath simple white crosses and Stars of David.

The volunteer G.I.s of today stand watch in Korea, the Persian Gulf, Europe, and the dangerous terrain of the Balkans. We must never see them as mere hirelings, off in a corner of our society. They are our best, and we owe them our full support and our sincerest thanks.

As the twentieth century closes, we look back to identify the great leaders and personalities of the past one hundred years. We do so in a world still troubled, but full of promise. That promise was gained by the young men and women of America who fought and died for freedom. Near the top of any listing of the most important people of the twentieth century must stand, in singular honor, the American G.I.

**Colin Powell**, former Chairman of the Joint Chiefs of Staff, is Secretary of State of the United States of America.

A hero is someone who has given his or her life to something bigger than oneself.

—Joseph Campbell, American teacher

I'm proud to be an American because Americans are the most generous people in the world.

I realize that this assertion runs right into the ugly face of the conventional wisdom of much of the elite in our country. They tell us that our country is permeated by individualism, that we have lost our old sense of community and civic responsibility, that our religion (dubbed by the critics "Sheliaism") is concerned only with self-fulfillment, that our social capital is in decline, and that we are greedy and selfish consumers.

Gimme a break!

As a sociologist my research shows that, as measured by proportion of income, Americans give more money to charities than does anyone else in the world. We are more likely than anyone else to engage in volunteer service, and our motives for volunteering are more likely to emphasize idealism than anyone else's. Our reasons for choosing our jobs and our careers are more likely to be based on generosity and service than reasons offered by people in other countries. As a country we funded the recovery of Europe and Japan after the war and continue to pour more money into the alleviation of misery than does any other country. Granted that there are still racism and discrimination in our country, can the critics name one European country where there aren't?

I have never been able to understand why America must be compared to some ideal and not at the same time compared to other real countries. Perhaps because those who make the comparisons are afraid that Americans will become complacent if they realize how good they really are. Perhaps they think that Americans will respond to the needs of others only if they are denounced.

It is a puzzle to me that so many people who should understand so much about human psychology are so clueless when appealing for more generosity.

There is much in the United States that needs to be improved. The most effective way to call forth even more generosity is to say, "We are the best there is, and, you know what, we have every intention of being even better!"

—Rev. Andrew M. Greeley
American sociologist

America has its faults as a society, as we have ours.

But I think of the Union of America born out of the defeat of slavery.

I think of its Constitution, with its unalienable rights granted to every citizen still a model for the world.

I think of a black man, born in poverty, who became chief of their armed forces and is now Secretary of State Colin Powell, and I wonder frankly whether such a thing could have happened here.

I think of the Statue of Liberty and how many refugees, migrants, and the impoverished passed its light and felt that if not for them, for their children, a New World could indeed be theirs.

I think of a country where people who do well don't have questions asked about their accent, their class, their beginnings but have admiration for what they have done and the success they've achieved.

I think of those New Yorkers I met, still in shock, but resolute: the firefighters and police, mourning their comrades but still heads held high.

I think of all this and I reflect: yes, America has its faults, but it is a free country, a democracy, it is our ally, and some of the reaction to September 11 betrays a hatred of America that shames those who feel it.

—Tony Blair, Prime Minister of
England, in a speech to the Labour Party
on October 2, 2001

# AMERICAN BEST

Have you not learned that not stocks or bonds or stately homes, or products of mill or field are our country? It is the splendid thought that is in our minds.

> —Benjamin Harrison
> Twenty-third President of the
> United States

## American Best—
## Variety, Optimism, Bounty, Talent:
## An Accounting

### BY ROGER ROSENBLATT

We celebrate ourselves and sing ourselves. We've sung ourselves so often we may have forgotten the reasons why. Open your eyes and take it in. The quiet little towns sit like drowsy dogs at the sides of the rivers. The city office buildings mirror one another in walls of blackened glass. Sing airport noises, freeway noises and broad smiles and arm-wrestling matches in a Minnesota diner with the President watching *Rocky* on TV and Bix Beiderbecke tooting blues in the corner. How about them Mets? O Kissinger. O Cher. The bellowing variety, the great mixed bag of nations. Of course we celebrate ourselves. The fact of our existence is reason enough to shout.

But can you pin it down precisely? [On the Fourth of July] a hundred million citizens will be cooing at the Statue of Liberty and popping Chinese firecrackers like machine guns far away. . . . Can anyone say why, exactly, we think we're special? After all, the Chinese made more than firecrackers, and the Greeks and Romans ran the world once too (not that we really do). In a heavenly accounting, those civilizations could provide a hefty list of what they offered to the world. If St. Peter asked Americans what they have offered, what would we say? Do car phones count?

In fact, the list of contributions is impressive, if something of a mess. We have our inventiveness to celebrate, our efficiency, the dollars. Old pluck and luck, hard work, can do. We have our generosity to celebrate, our respect for the rights of others, fair play—in principle, if not always in conduct. We celebrate the principle. National good nature; we have that to think about as well, and laughter at ourselves. "Don't get the idea that I'm one of these goddam radicals. Don't get the idea that I'm knocking the American system," said Al Capone. Celebrate the contradictions, the ironies. Celebrate the changes: the church becomes the bank becomes the alehouse becomes the madhouse becomes the whorehouse becomes the church. Celebrate the mobility, that we are a people in perpetual motion, whose motion is not aimlessness but optimism. A dreamy lot.

Some things are not to celebrate: the poor and desperate grow poorer and more desperate as the rich get richer. Children have children. Old industries grow feeble. Families dissolve. The waste. Illiteracy—here, where everyone is supposed to go to college. Ignorance, televised superstition, intolerance, race hatred, the discarding of the past. Almost every cause of shame is a consequence of the freedom that we celebrate above all things. Take the evil with the good, but keep the freedom; that's our motto. The trick is to spread the bounty of freedom around to correct the evil. When there is an effort to do that, one has something to celebrate. And still, can you pin it down? Sitting cross-legged on the green, sucking on your McDonald's vanilla shake, listening to the American Legion band play Dolly Parton songs on tubas, can you say what makes you feel different, special, pleased? Maybe it's because you are in a place where the self came to discover what it could do on its own. Because of an unspoken awareness that all people everywhere are alone with their possibilities and that you live where that fact, both the menace and the dram of it, is the message of the land. Because the country is inside you: better or worse as you are better or worse;

fairer, saner, kinder as you are any of those things. At night lie still and feel the struggles of your countrymen to make the progress of the nation fit the progress of their souls. They celebrate themselves and they sing themselves.

**Roger Rosenblatt**, award-winning essayist for *Time* magazine and PBS, is the author of several books including *Where We Stand: 30 Reasons for Loving Our Country.*

### Fifty Things Americans Like Best About Being American
BY MICHAEL LEACH AND FRIENDS

FROM SEA TO SHINING SEA

1. The Bill of Rights. All of them. Even the one you question. That's the point.
2. Having so many national heroes like George Washington, Abe Lincoln, and Rosa Parks, but having equal appreciation and respect for personal ones like a mother or father, a policeman or firefighter, a teacher or spouse.
3. A place that always welcomes new citizens to a better life. If not for that, we wouldn't be here.
4. A place where those who hate the change of seasons and those who love them can both find their perfect spots.
5. Churches, synagogues, mosques, and temples in every neighborhood in every city, and in every suburb and town.
6. The Rocky Mountains, especially Rocky Mountain National Park.
7. Tens of thousands of great lakes, and five really Great ones.
8. Shakespeare in the park every summer just about everywhere.
9. Steven Spielberg lives here.
10. E.T. used to live here.
11. Shirley MacLaine will live here again.
12. "The pursuit of happiness." No small thing. What other country acknowledges that Charlie Brown is Everyman?

13. Bob Dylan, Phil Ochs, Judy Collins, Buffy Sainte-Marie, Pete Seeger, Woody Guthrie, Peter, Paul and Mary, and other troubadors who taught us to sing about justice, to sing about free-ee-dom.

14. The Negro Spiritual.

15. Jazz—from Satchmo to Ella to Mingus and Sinatra.

16. Country music—George Strait, Loretta Lynn, Dolly Parton, and Indigo Girls.

17. Elvis will always live here.

18. All within a short plane ride: sunny beaches and snowcapped mountains; the Grand Canyon and the Grand Ole Opry; little cable cars and the Delta Queen; shining skyscrapers and fruited plains.

19. You wouldn't want to serve Maine lobster, red snapper, Cajun crawfish, and Alaskan king salmon as one meal, but in America you could.

20. In a college class you can find Christians of all stripes, Hindus, Muslims, Jews, Buddhists, atheists, Wicca advocates, and others, all capable of respectful conversation.

21. Your passport. A sign that you can travel almost anywhere you want with a basic freedom of movement to see and mix with your fellow human beings on our shared planet, and that you are not alone or unprotected: your country stands behind you and offers you havens of security—called U.S. embassies—around the world.

22. Sammy Sosa's smile.

23. Julia Roberts's smile.

24. Our smile when we behold Sammy Sosa or Julia Roberts.

25. "All men are created equal." Sure, some Americans have more money or power or fame than others, but even Bill Gates or George Bush or Oprah better not try to cut into the beer line at a ballgame.

26. *The Oprah Winfrey Show.* Proof that TV is capable of expressing spiritual values.

27. *The Jerry Springer Show.* Proof that the First Amendment is alive and well.

28. Being able to shank a golf ball, whiff a baseball, or shoot an airball, and still be invited to play the game.

29. The magnificent vulgarity of Las Vegas, the sublime majesty of the Golden Gate Bridge, the magisterial solemnity and dignity of Arlington National Cemetery.

30. Pulling together in a crisis—the Depression, World War II, gas shortages, September 11, or anytime one of our neighbors is in need.

31. Colin Powell lives here.

32. Abraham Lincoln lived here.

33. Our children and grandchildren get to live here.

34. Turkey, sweet potatoes, and family on Thanksgiving day.

35. Fireworks on the Fourth of July.

36. "The Star-Spangled Banner" sung at the World Series.

37. Thousands of retreat centers, monasteries, hermitages, religious camps, and refuges all over the country.

38. Mark Twain, Will Rogers, Dave Barry, Garrison Keillor, and Whoopi Goldberg. What other country is so good at laughter?

39. George Caleb Bingham, Georgia O'Keeffe, Edward Hopper, Grant Wood, indigenous artists who define our past.

40. The American G.I.

41. You can be a conscientious objector here.

42. You can criticize a politician and vote for him; you can contribute to a politician and vote against him; you can campaign for a politician and feel fulfilled even if he loses.

43. Paul Simon, the former senator from Illinois.

44. Paul Simon, the songwriter from New York.

45. Paul Simon, the grocer who lives in Milwaukee and has the same rights as the other Simons.

46. Where else can you fly across the country, land in so many different geographic and cultural environments, and never need a passport or go through customs?

47. The Lincoln Memorial. You don't have to know all it means to feel what it means.

48. The civil rights movement. What other country so readily acknowledges its grandest, most entrenched injustices and determinedly sets out to do something about them?

49. Ground Zero. The new monument, where the mystery of evil meets the mystery of love.

50. Before September 11 some people burned American flags. After September 11 you couldn't even buy one.

Ten Great American Values—or
Aunt Mary and Uncle Louie Are
Alive and Well and Living Next Door
BY MICHAEL LEACH

Sure, we Americans are materialistic, competitive, and preoccupied with how we feel. Nobody's perfect.

But at our best (and we're often at our best) we are a nation that cherishes and practices enduring values. Here are ten of them:

1. *Honesty and hard work.* My Uncle Louie, a construction worker, used to say: "An honest day's work for an honest day's dollar." That saying characterizes most Americans, whether our collars are blue or white or have rings around them. The average American is "Uncle Louie," a solid citizen who doesn't lie or steal or cheat because he values the Golden Rule. "Do unto others as you would have them do unto you" is tattooed on his soul.

2. *Generosity.* My Aunt Mary (who was half the size of Uncle Louie but had a heart as large as his toolbox) believed that "to whom much is given, much is expected." The average American is "Aunt Mary," a natural giver who complains about taxes and then writes a check for charity or helps someone down the block or halfway around the world without expecting anything in return. A Louis Harris survey shows that 73 percent of Generation Xers volunteer services to schools, charities, and churches. The acorns grow nicely, next to the tree.

3. *Fair play.* Uncle Louie wanted his team to win, his company to succeed, his children to prosper. But he eschewed the cliché "winning is everything," and bought into the one, "it's how you play the game that counts." That's what almost all of us teach our children, and that's why we're saddened when we read in the paper about someone doing the opposite. Like Uncle Louie we value getting ahead, but not at the expense of someone else. Those who break the rules make the headlines just because they are *not* the average American.

4. *Respect for differences.* Aunt Mary didn't like the new permissiveness but treated everyone who came into her house as she wanted to be treated, no matter what their opinions or habits. So what if she couldn't stop family members from arguing about Nixon or Kennedy at the table (even though she'd plead, "Please, no talking about politics or religion while we eat!"). Aunt Mary couldn't recite the Bill of Rights either. But she understood it: what demands respect is not the spoken word but the speaker.

5. *Family.* Of all the family values politicians talk about, the one dearest to the heart of Americans is the family itself. My Aunt Mary and Uncle Louie lived for their family. People everywhere hold marriage and family in high esteem. Americans value it so much that they throw up a million red flags in fear that it will disintegrate. Mount McKinley will go first.

6. *Self-reliance and responsibility.* Uncle Louie was a rugged individualist who worked with his hands and could rely on himself to get things done. He was also a union leader who participated with others in trying to make life better for everyone. Americans can go it alone when they have to, like war hero Audie Murphy who took out a bunker of enemy soldiers all by himself, or Michael Jordan who could win a basketball game just by willing it. But each of us knows that when we participate in a common cause for the good of all, we are at our best.

7. *Faith.* Skyscrapers now tower over church steeples as the highest points in the landscape, but hundreds of thousands of churches, temples, and mosques still anchor every neighborhood in every city, suburb, and town. We are founded on spiritual principles: that God created all of us in his image, that we are all equal in God's sight, and that we are each our brother's keeper. Almost 100 percent of Americans believe in God and pray in different ways. My Aunt Mary and Uncle Louie were devout Catholics. Aunt Mary had a shrine to Jesus, Mary, and the saints on her bedroom dresser that made St. Peter's in Rome look like a chapel. Uncle Louie never said much about his faith, just practiced it. They never argued about religion. Isn't this country grand?

8. *Ingenuity.* Uncle Louie drove cars that he kept going longer than dinosaurs ruled the earth. He could fix anything. Aunt Mary could take a

little pasta, oregano, tomato sauce, ricotta, and ground meat and create a feast to sate an army of chefs. Simple skills perhaps, but from the "Aunt Marys and Uncle Louies" of America have come more Nobel Prize–winning scientists than any country on earth. Their children have left footprints on the moon.

9. *Gratitude.* They didn't have a lot of material goods but they always had what they needed, and were grateful. Aunt Mary and Uncle Louie were thankful for so much, not least of which was being American. Why not? They lived in the only country on earth where Gratitude is a national holiday.

10. *Optimism.* Like everyone, Aunt Mary and Uncle Louie knew plenty of suffering in their lives but always held out hope that things would get better, even when they knew better. America is the land of optimism. "America," said playwright Dore Schary, "is a happy-ending nation." It doesn't always work out that way, but "Aunt Mary and Uncle Louie" assume that if the Declaration of Independence guarantees "the pursuit of happiness" as an unalienable right, surely its achievement is worth living for.

We're an imperfect people all right. But we are all "Aunt Mary and Uncle Louie," and our values are sound. So God bless the people next door. They are *you*!

> We must always remember that America is a great nation today not because of what government did for people but because of what people did for themselves and for one another.
> —Richard M. Nixon
> Thirty-seventh President of the
> United States

I was born in Chicago but when I was three months old my father took the family back to Sicily. I don't remember much of the old country but I have a vivid memory of when I was eight years old and we returned to America. I can still taste my first chocolate ice cream cone and my first peanut butter sandwich! They were wonderful!

And so were the people. I don't know who said it first but I learned early that in America you can depend on the kindness of strangers. The people are what is best about America.

—Sara Leach
Skokie, Illinois

The people next door: Aunt Mary and Uncle Louie with daughter, Genevieve, and son, Ronald.

Sara Giarrizzo Leach (the cute little baby who would grow up to marry Glen Leach, Chapter Seven) with her mother, father, brother, Charlie, and sister, Mary, who would later marry Uncle Louie.

You can't write about America without putting the word "kindness" in the first paragraph.

—Eric Hoffer, American philosopher

## A Great American Meal
### BY CHEF JEFF PEREZ

From apple pie to Yankee pot roast, from Boston clam chowder to Southern fried chicken, there are more delicious American meals than there are states in the Union. Here is a singular American feast that is easy to prepare and will satisfy the appetite of any American.

CALISTOGA SALAD

I got the inspiration for this salad during a trip to Calistoga in the Napa Valley, so a nice glass (or two) of Napa Valley chardonnay is required to fully enjoy this salad!

*Ingredients*
8 cups cleaned salad greens
1 cup crumbled gorgonzola cheese
½ cup red seedless grapes, halved
½ cup green seedless grapes, halved
2 apples, peeled, cored, and sliced
1 cup toasted walnuts
Your favorite salad dressing (oil and vinegar is preferred)

*Method*
Divide salad greens among four plates. Evenly divide the gorgonzola, grapes, apples, and walnuts among the four plates. Drizzle with your favorite salad dressing and enjoy!

THE BEST-EVER ROASTED CHICKEN

During the Great Depression, President Roosevelt promised a "chicken in every pot" for every American. Obviously he never tasted my roasted chicken!

*Ingredients*
One 3- to 3½-pound good-quality whole chicken
2 ounces of each: onion, celery, carrot roughly chopped
½ lemon
2 sprigs fresh rosemary
4 sprigs fresh thyme
½ bunch fresh parsley
2 ounces butter (room temperature)
Salt and pepper

*Method*
Preheat oven to 400. Stuff the cavity of the chicken with the celery, onion, carrot, and lemon. Chop all the fresh herbs and combine. Rub chicken with softened butter. Season the chicken with salt and pepper and rub with the chopped herbs. Roast the chicken until it has a nice brown color to the skin. Reduce oven temperature to 350 and continue cooking until the chicken is done, approximately one hour total cooking time.

SWEET POTATO SOUFFLÉ WITH PECAN STREUSEL

Sweet potatoes actually originated in Mexico and South and Central America. American Indians were growing them in the southern United States as early as 1540. The sweet potato was so important in the South that during the American Revolution and Civil War it was said to have sustained the armies.

*Soufflé Ingredients*
6 sweet potatoes
4 eggs beaten
4 ounces butter
1 cup milk
1 tablespoon butter

*Method*

Peel potatoes and cover with water. Simmer the potatoes until they can be easily pierced with a fork.

Drain and mash the potatoes. Add the eggs, 4 ounces of the butter, and the milk. Season with salt and pepper.

Rub the inside of an 8 × 11-inch baking dish with a tablespoon of the butter.

Spread the sweet potato mixture evenly in the baking pan and top with the streusel.

*Streusel Mix*
4 ounces butter
½ cup flour
1⅓ cup brown sugar
2 cups toasted pecans

*Method*

Place all ingredients in a bowl and mix by hand. Spread evenly on top of potato mixture. Bake at 350 until top is lightly browned and an internal temperature of 160 is reached. If streusel starts to brown too much, cover with foil. Rest for 15 minutes and serve.

## BOURBON-CRANBERRY BREAD PUDDING
## WITH VANILLA ICE CREAM

Bread pudding was discovered as a way to use stale bread and dates back to thirteenth-century England. It was then brought to America by the early colonists. I have added bourbon, the whiskey that is named after Bourbon County, Kentucky.

*Ingredients*
⅔ cup bourbon
1 cup heavy cream
3 cups milk
1¼ cups sugar
5 eggs
2 teaspoons vanilla extract

18 cups diced stale bread (no crust)
1 cup dried cranberries or raisins
1 teaspoon cinnamon
1 teaspoon nutmeg
Butter to grease baking pan

*Method*

Preheat oven to 350. Combine the bourbon, milk, cream, vanilla, sugar, eggs, dried cranberries, cinnamon, and nutmeg and whip together. Pour the mixture over the bread and allow to soak for approximately 30 minutes. Place the mixture in a buttered 8 × 8 baking dish and bake for about 45 minutes or until pudding is golden and puffy. Cool slightly and top with vanilla ice cream.

*Enjoy!*

**Chef Jeff Perez** is a certified chef de cuisine and executive chef at the Fairview Country Club, Greenwich, Connecticut.

# Chapter Nine

# THE AMERICAN DREAM

What does it mean to be American? If you work hard, things are definitely going to come to you. If you're a slacker, you'll get slacking results.

—Serena Williams, American tennis
champion, *Seventeen*

Even if you're poor, you're black, you're a refugee, and you don't know English—it doesn't matter in America. Here, if you work your butt off and don't give up, that's the key. When you've seen as much hardship and suffering as I have, studying hard isn't such a hardship. Where else but in America can someone with no money grow up and even get a scholarship and go to college?

—Mawi Asgedom, Harvard graduate,
escaped Ethiopia and fled a Sudanese
refugee camp with his family in
1983, author of *Beetles and Angels:
A Boy's Journey from a Refugee Camp
to Harvard*

"America is the land of opportunity!" he declared, as though I had just asked him what human beings really needed lungs for.

It was a wake-up call I'll never forget.

Fernando had been working in the university kitchen all day, as he did every day. Every weekend he worked as a janitor. I was a student and from modest circumstances myself, but my friend's Herculean labors inspired the question: Why, when he and his family had all they needed in Portugal—a home, good friends, and family—did they stay in the States and continue to endure so much hardship? Hadn't he had enough?

"America is the land of opportunity!"

I should have known better. How else, after all, to account for my own unlikely presence at the university—and as a graduate student, no less? Fernando was, I knew, not so different from the farm boys and factory workers I had gone to high school with—nor from my own truck-driving father who used a pocketknife to scrape clean his oil-stained fingernails on Sunday morning before the family went to Mass.

How could I forget? Two years earlier I couldn't decide whether to feel proud or angry when a priest friend told me he had used my life story in sermons: a so-called Cinderella story of a shy, skinny girl "escaping" (his word) this "hole" (his word again) of rural existence to become the cosmopolitan person I now seemed to be.

Like Fernando, both worlds make me who I am today and I love them both. My blood still boils when some people persist in misunderstanding and maligning rural life. But I also know how proud my grandma was to see me, the first in the family, get a college degree.

Either way, one thing is clear: I live in a country that makes it possible for both a Wisconsin native and a Portuguese immigrant to move from one world into another, to acquire an education independent of economic means, using both to fashion a lifestyle of one's choosing.

America *is* the land of opportunity.

Thank you, Fernando, for reminding me to be grateful for what has always been in front of my eyes.

—Mary Lynn Hendrickson
Chicago, Illinois

## The Birth of a Dream
BY DAN RATHER

*The Republic is a dream. Nothing happens unless first a dream.*
—Carl Sandburg

When we describe this land of ours, in deep-down essence and everyday spirit, it is the phrase we reach for most often. As an idea, it is older even than the nation and the words that give it name. It has reflected and informed what is best in us as a country and as a people from the beginning and it has been there to remind us that we should be doing better when we have failed to live up to the ideal it describes. It is the American dream, and it has filled me with awe for as long as I can remember.

I do not think it a stretch to call the American dream one of the most powerful ideas in the history of human achievement. As a young boy growing up in Houston, Texas, during the Great Depression, the dream was something taught by my parents. Not explicitly, but by example. By the way they lived their lives I grew to understand—could just *tell*—that it was something in which they were deeply and clearly invested. I could feel its truth in my father's tireless drive to build a better life for himself and his family and in my mother's determination to make the best of what we already had.

The dream kept them going through their dark hours, just as it sustained an entire nation of families—many worse than mine—through that time. And it also left a bitterness in the mouths of those Americans who had reached for it, brought it to their lips, and, like John Steinbeck's Joads, tasted nothing but dust. Such is the nature of dreams, when even dogged pursuit fails to catch them.

It was during this era of national trial, after the stock market crash and between the World Wars, that the historian James Truslow Adams became the first (so far as we can tell) to use the phrase, in an article he wrote in 1931 for the *Catholic Worker.* For him, the American dream was "the dream of a land in which life should be better and richer and fuller for every man, with opportunity for each according to his ability or achievement." The dream was, in short, the promise of freedom and opportunity.

**Dan Rather** is the anchor of the *CBS Evening News* and author of several books, including *The American Dream.*

I came to America in 1984 from Guyana, South America, with my wife and three daughters. I came to find freedom and opportunity, and miracle after miracle met me. I was a professional tailor and businessman, and within two months I was able to practice my trade again. All three of our daughters went to college, married, and gave us three American granddaughters. Last year I fulfilled a lifelong dream: my wife and I traveled to the land of our ancestors, India. America made these miracles possible, and I look forward to the next ones.

—Kissoon Singh
Pelham, New York

The American idea embraces a mysterious irony. Our founding fathers fought to expel the monarchy, yet as Americans we belong to a dynasty where we are each king and absolute ruler of our own destiny and desires, and where we can create our own American Dream.

—Joey Di Gioia
Stamford High School (Connecticut)

I grew up in a wonderful family in rural Mississippi, rich in love but not in worldly goods. My parents owned and operated a little bakery, and the only time they closed shop to take a break was Christmas. As a result, Christmas was a special time for them, especially my father, who loved the decorations and the carols.

They worked hard, year in and year out, to provide my four siblings and me with a good education so

"Daddy would tell us, 'I want you to go to college and get a good job.' "

that we wouldn't have to work as long and hard as they did. Daddy would scrape the sweat off his forearms with a spatula and tell us, "I don't want you to have to sweat like this. I want you to go to college and get a good job."

Not long after they retired and closed the bakery, my parents came to visit me in Washington where I was working in the White House as a Special Assistant to President Reagan. Because my daddy loved Christmas so much, I took him on a special tour of the State Rooms of the White House to see the beautiful decorations.

On the way back to my office in the Old Executive Office Building, we were walking through the basement of the West Wing. The place was deserted; most of my colleagues had left to begin their holidays.

As we were walking, one of the agents on the President's Secret Service detail hurried toward us, which meant the President was about to come through to go to a National Security Council meeting. I explained to the agent that we would like to stand to the side, out of the way, so my father could see the President. When President Reagan came through, he saw us standing there, stopped, and smiled. He came over, shook my father's hand, and said: "Mr. Jacobi, I want to thank you for making it possible for Mary Jo to be here. She's doing a wonderful job for our country."

My father was speechless and near tears. So was I. There was no greater Christmas gift that I could have given my daddy—then or since—than that special moment.

Where else could such a thing happen but in America?
—Mary Jo Jacobi
Bay St. Louis, Mississippi

I like being an American. To be an American, you stand up to be counted with Andrew Carnegie and Amelia Earhart, Jackson Pollock and Frank Lloyd Wright, Clara Barton and Helen Keller, Bill Gates and Dave Thomas, Lance Armstrong and Louis "Satchmo" Armstrong!

We are a nation of individualists. The dream that inspired millions of immigrants to forsake their homes and come to live here, despite poverty and want, still stands as a beacon for us today: we all have a chance to better ourselves. Nothing is as admired as the do-it-yourself story, the boy or girl who grew up in the gutter and went on to untold riches, climbing up the ladder rung by rung to the top, without sacrificing any principles. Read a Grisham novel and there it is—the young, dirt-poor lawyer who defeats the blueblood hot-shots in a heated courtroom battle. We love movies about the genius who rises up from the masses: *Goodwill Hunting, Finding Forrester.* Our heroes are the men and women who triumph over themselves and their circumstances to achieve personal greatness.

This is our heritage! We were founded by individualists longing to make their own choices. We were even obstinate enough to defeat the might of the British Empire during the American Revolution. Every settler here throughout our history was brave enough to say: "As safe as I am in my country, I long for more. I will sacrifice everything to live in a land where I may earn my living and choose my religion as I wish, because I am a human being and I deserve to be able to do so." America represents the triumph of human possibility. Inherent in our psyche is the knowledge that we are capable of great things, and inherent in our governmental structure is the license to pursue them. I am proud to live in a country that recognizes and respects the beauty and ability of a human being.

—Sarah Jacobi Tindall
New Orleans, Louisiana

What, after all, is the outstanding difference between Europe and America? What is the one thing beyond all others that strikes the visitor from the Old World as he travels about the New? Well, I will tell you; it is *youth*. The one great, challenging, striking, outstanding thing in America is the sense of youth everywhere. As a Londoner, the great outstanding difference that I find in America is the spirit of youth. In America everybody is young. Never mind what the calendar may say; here the heart is young. This is the outstanding difference, and it is also the secret of the American Dream, and the American achievement.

—Emmet Fox, *Alter Your Life*

I don't want to be a millionaire. I just want to live like one.
                                    —Toots Shor, American
                                    restaurateur–bon vivant

I'm not interested in money. I just want to be wonderful.
                                    —Marilyn Monroe, American actress

One day I came home and my parents were in the backyard and my
mother said, "How much is a dozen oranges?"

I knew.

"How much is a dozen eggs?"

And I knew. Because my father had a restaurant, so I knew the
prices.

And then they said, "How much is that breeze that's caressing
our faces? What do you think that sun is worth right now? And you
hear those birds? What's the price of those birds?"

They were trying to teach me that there are things that are price-
less. You don't always measure things by the dollar.

And I remembered that as I embarked on my struggle against
commercialism and the overwhelming spread of commercial dictates
into universities, into government, even into religion, into areas far
removed from traditional marketplace venues.
                                    —Ralph Nader
                                    American consumer activist

This is what is so interesting. In America, materialism is truly rampant and yet is on the way to the spirit. When a European becomes
a materialist, his or her human element dies. Americans are young
materialists. Actually, all children are materialists and then grow up
to what is not materialism. And so, crude American materialism will
develop directly into something spiritual. And this will come to pass
when the sun stands in the sign of Aquarius.
                                    —Rudolf Steiner, Austrian philosopher

The American dream isn't about the accumulation of material
things. It is much deeper and more profound than that. The essence

of the American dream is the understanding that we are here on this earth and in this land for a higher purpose: to discover—and develop to the fullest—our God-given potential. Anything that stands in the way of the dream, we must fight. Anything that enhances the dream, we must support.

—Steve Forbes, American businessman

I was born in Haifa, Israel. My mother and father were Hungarian Jews. My mother had been through the horrors of the German concentration camps. . . . Her entire family was killed in Nazi concentration camps. But she held her head high and kept instilling in me the notion that you should reach for your dreams. Coming to America really was an *Alice in Wonderland* experience. I remember seeing a poster of Santa Claus smoking Kent cigarettes. I'd never heard of Christ or Christmas or anything like that, and so I figured there's a rabbi, he's having a cigarette. America has been a hoot every day. I still see America as the promised land. . . .

—Gene Simmons (Kiss)
*New York Times Magazine*

I saw a sign at a gas station. It said, "Help Wanted." There was another sign below it that said "Self Service." So I hired myself. Then I made myself the boss. I gave myself a raise. I paid myself. Then I quit.

—Steven Wright, American comedian

*John Kinsella:* Is this heaven?
*Ray Kinsella:* It's Iowa.
*John Kinsella:* Iowa? I could have sworn this was heaven.
(*John starts to walk away.*)
*Ray Kinsella:* Is there a heaven?
*John Kinsella:* Oh yeah. It's the place where dreams come true.
(*Ray looks around, seeing his wife playing with their daughter on the porch.*)
*Ray Kinsella:* Maybe this is heaven.

—From the movie *Field of Dreams*
as transcribed on the Internet
Movie Data Base (www.imdb.com)

If you can dream it, you can do it.

—Walt Disney
American film producer

## Honoring the Dream
### BY LEE IACOCCA

When President Reagan asked me to serve as chairman of the Statue of Liberty–Ellis Island Centennial Commission, I was up to my ears at Chrysler. But I accepted anyway. People asked me: "Why did you take this on? Don't you have enough to do?"

But this was a labor of love for my father, who used to tell me about Ellis Island. My parents were greenhorns. They didn't know the language. They didn't know what to do when they came here. They were poor, and they had nothing. The island was part of my being—not the place itself, but what it stood for and how tough an experience it was.

But my getting involved in the restoration of these two great symbols is more than just a memorial to my parents. I, too, can identify with their experience. And now that I'm involved, I've found that almost every other American I meet feels the same way.

Those seventeen million people who passed through the gates of Ellis Island had a lot of babies. They gave America a hundred million descendants, which means that close to half of our country has its roots there.

And roots are what this country is yearning for. People are aching to return to basic values. Hard work, the dignity of labor, the fight for what's right—these are the things the Statue of Liberty and Ellis Island stand for.

Except for the American Indians, we're all immigrants or the children of immigrants. So it's important that we go beyond the stereotypes we've lived with. The Italians brought more to this country than pizza and spaghetti. The Jews brought more than bagels. The Germans brought more than knockwurst and beer. All the ethnic groups brought their culture, their music, their literature. They melted into the American pot—but somehow they also managed to keep their cultures intact as each rubbed off on the other.

Our parents came here and were part of the industrial revolution that changed the face of the world. Now there's a new high-tech revolution and everyone's scared out of their wits. When you're in a mode of change, as we're in right now, the great fear is that a lot of people might just turn out to be you. That's why so many people are worried. They're asking themselves: "Will we be as good as our parents in coping with these new changes, or will we be left out in the cold?" And our kids are beginning to ask: "Do we have to lower our expectations and our standard of living?"

Well, I want to say to them: It doesn't have to be that way. If our grandparents could overcome, maybe you can, too. You may never have thought about it, but they went through hell. They gave up a lot. They wanted your life to be better than theirs.

When the chips were down, my mother found nothing wrong with working in the silk mills so I could have lunch money for school. She did what she had to do. When I got to Chrysler I found a royal mess, but I did what I had to do.

Think about it. The last fifty years can give you a vision for the next fifty. What the last fifty years taught us was the difference between right and wrong, that only hard work succeeds, that there are no free lunches, that you've got to be productive. Those are the values that made this country great.

And those are the values that the Statue of Liberty represents. The Statue of Liberty is just that—a beautiful symbol of what it means to be free. The reality is Ellis Island. Freedom is just the ticket of admission, but if you want to survive and prosper, there is a price to pay.

I've had a terrific career, and this is the country that gave me the chance to do it. I seized the opportunity, but I was no ninety-day wonder. It took me almost forty years of hard work.

People say to me: "You're a roaring success. How did you do it?" I go back to what my parents taught me. Apply yourself. Get all the education you can, but then, by God, *do* something! Don't just stand there, make something happen. It isn't easy, but if you keep your nose to the grindstone and work at it, it's amazing how in a free society you can become as great as you want to be. And, of course, also be grateful for whatever blessings God bestows on you.

**Lee Iacocca,** the son of immigrants, was a straight-shooting businessman who has become a symbol of integrity and know-how for millions of Americans. His autobiography, *Iacocca,* has 7 million copies in print.

Today millions of Americans, the quiet Americans, the selfless Americans, are giving of their time and themselves, and they work at day-care centers and inner-city schools, homes for the elderly—anywhere there's a need, anytime they are needed—making a difference in the lives of those for whom the American dream seems an impossible dream.

—George Bush
Forty-first President of the
United States

Blind faith in the American dream led my grandparents from the eastern coast of Italy to Ellis Island. Without the benefit of language lessons or translator machines, they made the courageous decision to immigrate. They left their homes, jobs, and families to make a harrowing journey across the ocean, bringing with them only what they could carry. They came to this land without the ability to speak the language, without knowledge of the customs, and without money. They had no homes and no jobs, but somehow, despite these circumstances, they made it—they made it here in America. They not only made it, they helped make America what it is today: the greatest nation in the world. And I thank God they did, because if it were not for them, I wouldn't be here, my kids wouldn't be here, and their kids as well. Today we all have so much to be thankful for—not only the sacrifices our ancestors made, but to the country that adopted us and said "Benvenuto!" as we landed on its shores. God bless America!

—Joseph R. Cerrell, President of the
National Italian-American
Foundation Los Angeles, California

My parents found here a compassionate land and a compassionate people. They found a government that protected their labor, educated their children, and provided help to those of their fellow citizens who were in need. They found their dream in America and they passed that dream on to their children.

—Colin Powell, U.S. Secretary of State

If we look to the answer as to why for so many years we achieved so much, prospered as no other people on earth, it was because here in this land we unleashed the energy and individual genius of man to a greater extent than has ever been done before. Freedom and dignity of the individual have been more available and assured here than in any other place on earth.

—Ronald Reagan
Fortieth President of the
United States

Liberty, when it begins to take root, is a plant of rapid growth.

—George Washington
First President of the United States

## The American Language

In Europe languages had made nations. Spanish, Portuguese, English, French, German, and Italian had produced their own literatures—even before there was a Spain, a Portugal, an England, a France, a Germany, or an Italy. But the United States was the first great modern nation without its own language. Our country has been uniquely created by people willing and able to borrow a language.

Oddly enough, the English language has helped make us a congenitally multicultural nation, since most Americans have not come from the land of Shakespeare. So we have learned here that people do not lose their civic dignity by speaking the language of a new community. The English language has been invigorated and Americanized by countless importations of words from German, Italian, French, Spanish, Yiddish, and American Indian tongues, among others.

The surprising result is that, without a unique national language, our community has developed a language wonderfully expressive of the vitality and variety of our people. Perhaps we should really call Broken English our distinctive American language, for it bears the mark of our immigrant history.

—Daniel J. Boorstin
American historian, *Parade*

I don't mean to offend my friends back in my native England but I must say: to enjoy English as a living language come to America! The English Departments of American universities are the safekeepers of our language. There we find the scholars, descendants of immigrants not only from the British Isles but from Eastern Europe to Korea, individuals from all over the globe who have made this wonderful language their own. These preservers of our rich legacy leave their ivory towers and mingle and interact with the rest of us on a daily basis, enhancing our own appreciation of the language. Then society at large feeds back into the system with fresh words to enliven that same English. Who would be without boondoggle, gee whiz, inner city, vigilante, yuppie, and zipper, to name a few examples? It gives me immense satisfaction to be part of this process. Reading the Declaration of Independence is a particular pleasure!

—Arthur Quinton
Amherst, Massachusetts

Chapter Ten

# AMERICAN CULTURE

*Cynics would say that American culture is an oxymoron. Cynics are morons.*

*We can't help it if people all over the world want to see our movies and read our books and even watch our silly television shows. We are the first to admit that much of what passes for popular culture is mind candy. After all, that's why we invented the clicker, not to mention the multiplex and the superstore. America is all about choices.*

*But look around. And listen up. You'll hear jazz and the blues. See the Chicago skyline and Lincoln Center. Experience free concerts in the park every spring and summer from Maine to Malibu. Art and culture in the forms of music, dance, the-ater, architecture, painting, film, and literature are everywhere and available to everyone. We Americans buy more books than any other country in the world. So what if Richard Simmons writes a lot of them. We also exercise the most.*

*The "ten best" lists in this chapter are just for fun. They don't pretend to be the best American books or movies or songs but are select examples that best re-flect what it means to be an American—and that do so with a measure of art and grace. They are strictly personal. If you disagree, make your own list.*

*It's easy. There is so much to choose from!*

### The Ten Best Books About Being American You'll Ever Read
BY EVANDER LOMKE

1. *Uncle Tom's Cabin; or, The Man that Was a Thing* (1852), by Harriet Beecher Stowe. Its publication was an unparalleled event in the history of the

novel, making Stowe the most famous writer of her time. Her characters, such as Simon Legree (the Southern slave owner originally from Vermont), Uncle Tom, Sambo, Little Eva, and Topsy, have taken on the mantle of universality. Speaking of the Civil War, Abraham Lincoln greeted Stowe as "the little lady who made this big war" and thus opened the doors of racial equality. Her great book on our nation's shameful enslavement of African Americans has been translated into forty languages and was hailed by contemporary European intellectuals as diverse as Heinrich Heine and George Sand.

2. *Self-Reliance* (1841, 1847) by Ralph Waldo Emerson. This is America's greatest nonfiction writer's greatest work. We are granted our innate freedom by God; but it is up to each of us to use this freedom wisely. *"Trust thyself. 'How do you know it is truth?' We know truth when we see it."* Has anyone better articulated the inner light of freedom, freedom's responsibilities, and, therefore, what it truly means to be an American? This Transcendentalist classic has also served as a model for a uniquely American form of spirituality and self-help that is evident in the books of spiritual pioneers, preachers, and authors from Mary Baker Eddy to Norman Vincent Peale to countless other bestselling writers today.

3. *The Rights of Man* (1791, 1792) by Thomas Paine. Paine was a revolutionary among revolutionaries, whose writings prove that the pen is mightier than the sword. His work was especially promoted by Thomas Jefferson, with whom Paine had a long and fruitful correspondence. Paine's pamphlets are notable for their disarming simplicity of expression (he wrote an equally famous one on *Common Sense)* combined with depth of thought. They appealed to the average person in the championing of reason over despotism. For Paine, the old monarchical dispensation had passed: America represents a shining new epoch in the history of the world. Few works so forcefully express the universal ideals of Life, Liberty, and the pursuit of Happiness.

4. *Call It Sleep* (1934) by Henry Roth. Emma Lazarus's "The New Colossus" (1883) beautifully evokes the rich ethnic backdrop of the once-primarily Jewish ghettoes of Brownsville and the Lower East Side as seen through the eyes of a sensitive boy: *"Give me your tired, your poor,/ Your huddled masses*

*yearning to breathe free,/ The wretched refuse of your teeming shore,/ Send these, the homeless, tempest-tost to me:/ I lift my lamp beside the golden door."* Roth's heartfelt book was largely overlooked for thirty years, when it was rediscovered as an American masterpiece. What is the meaning of life? It is the peace that comes with acceptance. ONE MIGHT AS WELL CALL IT SLEEP the young narrator realizes by the conclusion of a novel that is one of the most distinctive and unforgettable ever written on the twentieth-century urban-American immigrant experience.

5. *Adventures of Huckleberry Finn* (1884, 1885) by Samuel Langhorne Clemens (Mark Twain). Here is a case of the sequel being better than the original *(The Adventures of Tom Sawyer)*. No less an authority than Ernest Hemingway considered *Adventures of Huckleberry Finn* the source of all American writing, while William Dean Howells called its author "the Lincoln of our literature." Society's ultimate outsiders, Huck Finn, who is abused by his alcoholic father, and the runaway slave Jim humbly sail their raft down the Mississippi River and into the imagination of every American. Along the way, they encounter every personality a continent can hold. Through this novel, Mark Twain cast his clear sight both on the great eastern establishment and westward, as well as on racism in its many guises. *Huckleberry Finn* is simultaneously a nostalgic account of childhood, a satire and a stern social and moral record of our country and way of life.

6. *The Catcher in the Rye* (1951) by J. D. Salinger. Sixteen-year-old Holden Caulfield is Huckleberry Finn by way of Sigmund Freud. These are the years after World War II, when Americans were desperately trying to put their lives back together. Like Clemens's hero, but in an upper-middle-class, atomic-age context, Holden is the prototypical, existential American loner and outsider. Yet, paradoxically, he is also the inner voice of teens and all adults still sensitive to those formative years. Holden's Christmastime holiday in New York, and attempts to come to grips with everything that is "phony" in his world, make this novel as meaningful and popular fifty years after publication as it was for a nation in the grip of the cold war.

7. *Leaves of Grass* (nine editions between 1855 and 1892) by Walt Whitman. This collection, which Whitman continually reworked and added to over his

lifetime, is the visionary, free-verse wellspring of the American poetic spirit: *"I bequeath myself to the dirt to grow from the grass I love. / You hardly know who I am or what I mean, / But I shall be good health to you nevertheless. . . . / Failing to fetch me at first keep encouraged, / Missing me one place search another, / I stop somewhere waiting for you."* Through "Song of Myself," "I Sing the Body Electric," "Drum-Taps," "O Captain! My Captain!" and "When Lilacs Last in the Dooryard Bloom'd," many appearing in subsequent editions of *Leaves of Grass,* Whitman's is *the* transcendent American poetic voice. His genius was to record and distill the American worldview of individual freedom through the Civil War and some of history's darkest hours.

8. *The Story of My Life* (1902) by Helen Keller. Do you believe in miracles? In miracle workers? Reared in Alabama, deaf and blind from infancy, Helen Keller recounts the work and inspiration of her teacher, Annie Sullivan; her love of the blind poet Homer as well as Mark Twain; and her hatred of racial prejudice. Anyone psychologically paralyzed by self-absorption, feeling exiled from all happiness and hope, stuck in self-pity (and who isn't from time to time?) will draw courage from this amazing story of personal triumph over disability. In the spirit of America, Helen Keller was not born to greatness: but she overcame unimaginable obstacles and odds to make herself great, and then to help others.

9. *Black Boy* (1945) by Richard Wright. One of the magnificent, unflinching autobiographies that reads like a novel, this is a story of growing up in the South up to the age of nineteen with the narrator's move to Chicago. Through the voracious reading of (mostly white) authors, and his own keen observations of place, Wright recounts how he pulled himself out of racist poverty and life in a dysfunctional home. This powerful book is at far remove from Stowe's depiction of a certain form of slave life in *Uncle Tom's Cabin* (Wright's first collection is called *Uncle Tom's Children*) or the masked-slave narratives of Joel Chandler Harris's *Uncle Remus: His Songs and His Sayings* (1881). Amazingly, Wright's entire work, *American Hunger,* of which *Black Boy* is the first part, was not published until 1992.

10. *The Greatest Generation* (1998) by Tom Brokaw. A news anchor becomes caught in his own anniversary-news story on the D-Day invasion that began

the liberation of Europe and also formed today's America. Here are the lives of so-called ordinary citizens as well as the rich and famous of the Greatest Generation, who saved the democracy we cherish, more than sixty years later, from the Great Depression and World War II. A kind of extended-family album, this book is above all a compelling lesson in self-sacrifice and service to country. It is about the quiet inner hero of every American man and woman who, when called upon, appeared in a single generation that is now passing from our sight if not our hearts and memory.

*Honorable Mentions*

*Moby-Dick; or, The Whale* (1851), by Herman Melville. This book is generally acknowledged as the Great American Novel even though it has no women, revolves around timeless biblical themes and images that long preceded the existence of the United States, and is largely a Great American Quest set on the high seas far from our shores. The Everyman narrator, Ishmael, recounts the maimed Captain Ahab's tragic revenge on the white whale, Moby Dick. What part of the American psyche Ahab and this whale actually represent, and what Melville means by it all, have teased and eluded readers for generations.

*The Yearling* (1938) by Marjorie Kinnan Rawlings. There could not be a more different "animal tale" from *Moby-Dick* than this magical Pulitzer Prize–winning novel. As a coming-of-age story, the book depicts thirteen months of a boy's life in rural-northern Florida during the early 1870s. It is about Jody Baxter and his pet fawn, Flag. Jody comes to learn the toil and hard realities of his family's existence when he is forced to kill his beloved pet who has been eating their crops, and is only reconciled with his father after much heartache. The edition illustrated in full color by N. C. Wyeth is stunning. (*Moby-Dick* and *The Yearling* were made into memorable films, in 1956 and 1946 respectively, both starring Gregory Peck.)

*Democracy in America* (1835, 1840) by Alexis Charles Henri Maurice Clérel de Tocqueville and *Notions of the Americans Picked up by a Travelling Bachelor* (1828) by James Fenimore Cooper (tie). Tocqueville was a young French aristocrat commissioned to study the prison system in this country. In the course of his tour he wrote the first, surprisingly nuanced, sociological study of American life and our democracy. Far less known is Cooper's almost contemporaneous American travel book. The narrator is a fictionalized European who meets an American gentleman functioning as an "interpreter" of his country. Cooper's book is filled both with faith in our boundless energies as well as almost miraculous predictions, including one that figures a U.S. population of 200 million by 1980!

*The Virginian* (1902) by Owen Wister. Zane Grey and Louis L'Amour, Cormac McCarthy and Larry McMurtry would probably not have had the same writing careers were it not for Owen Wister. An aristocratic Harvard-educated social critic, Wister found himself falling in love with the West he had visited for purposes of improving his health. Wister single-handedly invented the lore of the cowboy—the maverick amid the vast American West—in one book. "Turn your face to the great West, and there build up a home and fortune," said Horace Greeley prophetically, some fifty years before *The Virginian* was published.

*The Glory of Their Times* (1966, 1984) by Lawrence S. Ritter. This is the most passionate, lyrical, and truly nostalgic of all the books on America's favorite pastime. Like an anthropologist, Ritter transcribed tape-recorded reminiscences of major-league ballplayers, famous and not (but white only, as the major leagues were at the time) from a long-ago era, as they reflect, as old men, on the greatness of the game they love. Played through several wars, economic depressions, and national crises, baseball and its defining ingredient, its lore, are nowhere on finer literary display.

**Evander Lomke** of New York City is managing editor of *The Continuum Encyclopedia of American Literature.*

The Americans of all nations at any time upon the earth have probably the fullest poetical nature. The United States themselves are essentially the greatest poem. In the history of the earth hitherto the largest and most stirring appear tame and orderly to their ampler largeness and stir. Here at last is something in the doing of man that corresponds with the broadcast doings of the day and night. Here is not merely a nation but a teeming nation of nations.

—Preface to *Leaves of Grass*
by Walt Whitman

## The Ten Best Movies About Being American You'll Ever See

BY MICHAEL LEACH

1. *It's a Wonderful Life* (1946). Jimmy Stewart, more than any other actor, embodied American values. In movies like *Mr. Smith Goes to Washington, The Spirit of St. Louis,* and, most of all, *It's a Wonderful Life,* he showed us our best side. In this life-affirming story of second chances (and who hasn't seen it at

"Look, Daddy . . . every time a bell rings an angel gets his wings!" Still from *It's a Wonderful Life* autographed by Karolyn Grimes (Zuzu Bailey).

least three times?), Jimmy's character, George Bailey, inspires us to be our best selves. He values family and friends over fame and fortune, but when trouble strikes, as it inevitably does, he questions the meaning of his life. Director Frank Capra asks, "What would the world be like if he—or you—had never been born?" and his movie answers, "A sorry place indeed." The same could be said of the America that Jimmy Stewart represents. Whether you watch this Christmas classic on December 24 or on the Fourth of July, you will feel grateful for your blessings and want to share them with others.

2. *The Grapes of Wrath* (1940). Henry Fonda is Tom Joad in this masterpiece about a migrant family during the Great Depression. Directed by John Ford from a novel by John Steinbeck, it makes us taste the dust of poverty and appreciate our oneness with the least of us. We learn that Tom Joad's family is our family and how important this truth is to the soul of our country. At the end Fonda must flee from the law and leave his family. But he's on to something. "Maybe it's like Casey says," he tells his mother. "A fellow ain't got a soul of his own, just a little piece of a big soul, the one big soul that belongs to everybody . . . then . . . I'll be everywhere, wherever you can look! Wherever there's a fight so hungry people can eat, I'll be there. Wherever there's a cop beatin' up a guy, I'll be there. I'll be in the way guys yell when they're mad. I'll be in the way kids laugh when they're hungry and they know supper's ready and where people are eatin' the stuff they raise and livin' in the houses they build. I'll be there, too." And so will you!

3. *Little Big Man* (1970). Native Americans have always known that we are all pieces of one great soul. Twenty years before Kevin Costner danced with wolves, Dustin Hoffman played a white man who was raised by Indians and moved through both cultures for more than a hundred years. Based on a novel by Thomas Berger and directed by Arthur Penn, *Little Big Man* shows Native Americans as "human beings" for perhaps the first time in film. One of them observes: "There is an endless supply of white men. But there has always been a limited number of 'human beings.' We won today, we won't win tomorrow." *Little Big Man* is at once a satire and an antidote that requires our attention; it suggests "how the West was lost."

4. *Glory* (1989). Matthew Broderick is superb as Colonel Robert Shaw, a white Bostonian who led the first black regiment during the Civil War and

overcame prejudice from both his superiors and his men. Denzel Washington won an Academy Award as Trip, an angry runaway slave who found family in the band of brothers that was "the 54th." *Glory*, while told mostly through the viewpoint of Colonel Shaw, is a moving testament to men who lived and died—together—for freedom.

5. *Avalon* (1990). "I came to America in 1914 by way of Philadelphia. That's where I got off the boat. And then I came to Baltimore. It was the most beautiful place you've ever seen in your life. There were lights everywhere. What lights they had! It was a celebration of lights! I thought they were for me, Sam, who was in America. Sam was in America! It was the Fourth of July!" So begins director Barry Levinson's loving album of three generations in a family much like his own. *Avalon* is a loving tribute to immigrant families at the turn of the century and to their descendants as well.

6. *Field of Dreams* (1989). "If you believe the impossible," said the movie poster, "the incredible can come true." What could be more American than that? Kevin Costner looks for the American dream in Iowa. He hears a voice telling him to build a baseball field. He listens. He builds. And they come: the Chicago Black Sox, his father, the world. *Field of Dreams* is about re-creating the past and making it whole, about forgiveness and rebirth, about baseball and Iowa—essential patches from the American quilt.

7. *Hoosiers* (1986). Gene Hackman plays a down-on-his-luck basketball coach who comes to a small Indiana town and leads the high school team to the state finals in 1954. He redeems not only himself but the town drunk, and wins the love of Barbara Hershey. Based on a true story, *Hoosiers* is about believing in yourself, coming back and starting over, basketball, and Indiana—more beautiful pieces from the American quilt.

8. *Saving Private Ryan* (1998). Steven Spielberg makes us feel the horror of battle and the values of courage, leadership, and, most important, gratitude. Spielberg is the only filmmaker to consistently hold high the virtue of gratitude: at the end of *Schindler's List*, survivors place stones of thanks on Schindler's grave, and at the end of this film Ryan visits the tomb of the man who saved him and falls down in tears of thanksgiving. *Saving Private Ryan* bursts with as much American spirit as the sky on the Fourth of July.

9. *High Noon* (1952). Gary Cooper played Sergeant York, Lou Gehrig, and Mr. Deeds. Here he is Marshal Will Kane, a man who gives definitive meaning to the term "self-reliance." Bad guys are coming to tear up the town and "shoot him dead" and none of the townsfolk will lend a hand. Cooper, a man of honor, refuses to leave his post. In an exciting climax Coop triumphs and leaves with his honor intact, and with Grace Kelly holding his wounded arm. Shot in real time, and with a haunting score ("Do Not Forsake Me, O My Darling"), *High Noon* gave definitive meaning to a new genre called "the adult Western."

10. *The Right Stuff* (1983). Based on a book by journalist Tom Wolfe, this epic set in the late fifties is about American heroes—and how the media manufacture public heroes out of private ones. The movie contrasts flier Chuck Yeager, who does amazing feats when no one is watching, with the first astronauts chosen by the government to be poster boys in the space race. The irony is that the astronauts, like Yeager, have the "right stuff" but often choose illusion over reality for a greater good. The film suggests that that takes the "right stuff," too. A soaring score by Bill Conti *(Rocky)* and others makes you shiver red, white, and blue all over.

*Honorable Mentions*

*Yankee Doodle Dandy* (1942). Jimmy Cagney plays patriotic song and dance man George M. Cohan with such gusto that we can only say what he said: "My father thanks you, my mother thanks you, my sister thanks you, and I assure you that I thank you!"

*Malcolm X* (1992). In what may be the most authentic story of religious conversion ever made, Denzel Washington becomes the controversial and inspiring black leader of the 1960s. To walk in his shoes is to walk in the shoes of many black Americans before and during the civil rights era and, like Malcolm at the end of his life, to hunger for reconciliation.

*Twelve Angry Men* (1957). Just twelve members of a jury in one sweltering room, but one of them is Henry Fonda, and he leads them in the pursuit of truth in this riveting tribute to the American justice system.

*To Kill a Mockingbird* (1962). Gregory Peck is Atticus Finch, a small-town lawyer who embodies American values and a parent who loves his children and teaches them those values in this heartwarming rendition of Harper Lee's beloved novel.

*The Color Purple* (1985). Directed by Steven Spielberg from the Pulitzer Prize–winning novel by Alice Walker, *The Color Purple* affirms the indomitable spirit of women and the worth of every human being. Who could ask for anything more?

*1776* (1972). A musical about the signing of the Declaration of Independence? It may be as corny as Kansas in August but it's also informative and inspiring in a most unusual way. Well worth watching every Fourth of July.

*The Wizard of Oz* (1939). "Toto, we're home! Home! And this is my room, and you're all here. And I'm not gonna leave here ever, ever again, because I love you all, and—oh, Auntie Em—there's no place like home!"

"The one constant through all the years, Ray, has been baseball. America has rolled by like an army of steamrollers. It's been erased like a blackboard, rebuilt, and erased again. But baseball has marked the time. This field, this game, is a part of our past, Ray. It reminds us of all that once was good, and that could be again. Oh, people will come, Ray. People will definitely come!"

—James Earl Jones as Terrence Mann
in *Field of Dreams*

### The Top Ten Songs That Celebrate America
BY JOSEPH DUREPOS

1. *The Star-Spangled Banner.* Written by Francis Scott Key in 1814 when he sighted the American flag still waving at dawn after the British attack on Fort

McHenry, Baltimore, Maryland. Congress declared it our official National Anthem on March 3, 1931. Although written almost two hundred years ago, this song made many of us weep in the wake of the September 11 attacks; the picture of the three firefighters raising the flag in the dust and rubble is our most vividly patriotic image since the Marines on Iwo Jima during World War II.

2. *America the Beautiful.* After climbing Pike's Peak in Colorado in 1895 and viewing the "spacious skies," Katharine Lee Bates wrote this as a poem. The lyrics were later set to music from the hymn *Materna,* which had been written several years earlier by Samuel Augustus Ward. This soaring song of praise vivifies the vastness and splendor that is America. "America! America! God shed His grace on thee, and crown thy good with brotherhood from sea to shining sea!" These nineteen words encourage feelings of gratitude in all of us.

3. *God Bless America.* Written by Irving Berlin in 1917 for a musical but shelved for two decades until Kate Smith performed it on radio in 1938. From that moment on the song became an emotional standard-bearer for Americans during World War II and beyond. "God bless America, my home sweet home." Part invocation, part celebration, this wonderful composition is as well known and loved as any patriotic song in our nation's history.

4. *America/My Country 'Tis of Thee.* Lyrics written by Samuel Francis Smith in 1832 to the tune of *God Save the King.* Sung by schoolchildren for many years as a complement to the Pledge of Allegiance. Who of us doesn't remember as a child, holding our hand to our chest, and coming to understand—even if dimly—something of what it means to be an American at the start of each new day?

5. *Battle Hymn of the Republic.* Julia Ward Howe wrote the words in 1862 while watching the Union Army in review singing *John Brown's Body,* a tune written, interestingly enough, by Southern composer William Steffe. First published in *The Atlantic Monthly,* it became the semiofficial Civil War song of the North. This glorious and stirring song with its repeating verse of "Glory! Glory! Hallelujah! Glory! Glory! Hallelujah! Glory! Glory! Hal-

lelujah! His truth is marching on," is one more example of a songwriter's belief that America's fortunes are tied to God's providence.

6. *Dixie.* Ironically, in 1860, New Yorker Dan Emmett wrote what would become the semiofficial song of the Confederacy after complaining about the Northern weather. The song went on to worldwide acclaim and was popular on both sides of the Civil War. "I wish I was in Dixie" was such a popular refrain that Abraham Lincoln declared *Dixie* a spoil of war and claimed it for the united country.

7. *Amazing Grace.* John Newton, a wealthy slave trader, was caught in a storm during an Atlantic crossing. He prayed to God that if salvation could come to "a wretch like me" he would change his life. He kept his word and became a passionate abolitionist and Methodist minister. He composed the hymn sometime between 1760 and 1770. Who has not been moved by its feelings of mercy and redemption? Every time I hear it, no matter the version, I sense the promise that America represents—a fresh start, a new beginning, with God's help.

8. *God Bless the USA.* Words and music by Lee Greenwood in 1985. Greenwood won the Country Music Award for Song of the Year that same year for this modern patriotic classic. It was during and after the Gulf War in 1991 that Greenwood's song became a favorite of our armed forces. Since then, he has toured extensively with the USO in support of America's peacekeepers all over the world. The song has taken on a special poignancy in the wake of September 11. Millions of listeners have found comfort and hope in these words: "If tomorrow all the things were gone I'd worked for all my life, and I had to start again with just my children and my wife, I'd thank my lucky stars to be living here today, 'cause the flag still stands for freedom and they can't take that away."

9. *Yankee Doodle.* This simple ditty, written by Dr. Richard Shuckburg in 1765, became popular during the French and Indian Wars. Later it became an anthem for both sides of the conflict in the Revolutionary War. When the Continental Army sang it mockingly at the British troops surrendering with General Cornwallis to General George Washington, it became an American standard.

10. *Coming to America.* Written and first sung by Neil Diamond in 1980. Go ahead, try and tell me this song of the immigrant's dreams of a New World doesn't touch you! You'd be lying.

**Joseph Durepos,** senior editor of trade books for Loyola Press, listens to music in Downers Grove, Illinois.

## Fourteen Great American Composers
### BY DAVID GOODNOUGH

1. *Samuel Barber* (1910–81) is best known for his *Adagio for Strings,* perhaps one of the most moving pieces of music ever written. His concertos for violin and piano are among the greatest of the past century. His opera *Vanessa* has been performed by the world's leading opera companies, and his *Antony and Cleopatra* was premiered by the Metropolitan Opera in 1966 at the opening of its new house in Lincoln Center. An accomplished singer himself, Barber wrote some two hundred songs, including the achingly nostalgic *Knoxville: Summer of 1915.*

2. *Amy Beach* (1867–1944). Her *Gaelic Symphony* (1896) was the first symphony composed by an American woman. More than 150 works, including a piano concerto, chamber music, choral pieces, and songs reveal a complete mastery of the musical expression of her times. She was a famed concert pianist and a tireless promoter of her own works as well as her contemporaries'. Once hailed as the foremost woman composer in America, if not, indeed, the world, her music is now being revived due to an increased interest in late-nineteenth-century American music and in the work of women composers.

3. *Leonard Bernstein* (1918–90), America's first truly great conductor, a television star, a writer, a teacher, and an international celebrity. All of his accomplishments began with his compositions. Best known for his works for the theater such as *West Side Story,* he also found time to write large orchestral pieces, including two symphonies, choral works, and songs. His *Candide Overture* is the most frequently performed work by an American composer worldwide.

4. *Aaron Copland* (1900–90) is America's greatest composer, period. His Third Symphony is the standard by which all others must be judged. His ballet scores, particularly *Appalachian Spring,* created an American sound that is now recognized as unique to this country. His "difficult" music has earned him as much respect among serious musicians and scholars as his more accessible works have among the general public. His *Fanfare for the Common Man* is so familiar and so American-rooted that some listeners mistake it for a folk tune or a traditional hymn.

5. *George Gershwin* (1898–1937) is America's most beloved composer, to whose music just about everyone can relate. With *Rhapsody in Blue* he introduced a new idiom to concert music—jazz—his use of which has never been surpassed. His massive *Concerto in F* remains the most-played American piano concerto, and every one of his orchestral works, most notably *An American in Paris,* has entered the repertory of major symphony orchestras. Even some of his Broadway show songs have crossed over into concert performance, and his *Porgy and Bess* is still the greatest American opera.

6. *Louis Moreau Gottschalk* (1829–69) was America's first ambassador of music. He was known throughout Europe for his piano virtuosity and his compositions, notably the *Louisiana Trilogy,* which drew heavily on the creole music of his native New Orleans. He traveled extensively in Europe and South America, performing and composing. Best known for his piano works, he also wrote for large orchestra, most notably his symphony *Night in the Tropics* and *Grand Tarantelle* for piano and orchestra. But he will forever be identified with the Cakewalk.

7. *Howard Hanson* (1896–1981). Hailing from Wahoo, Nebraska, he is difficult to place in Rome, where he studied, or the capitals of Europe, where he toured to great acclaim with his own Eastman-Rochester Orchestra. One of the great teacher-composers, he headed the Eastman School of Music for forty years, but found time to write seven symphonies, instrumental works in almost every form, choral works, and an opera, *Merry Mount,* one of the few operas with a wholly American subject produced by the Metropolitan Opera. He is best known for his Second Symphony *(Romantic),* the suite from his opera, and *Drum Taps,* choral settings for poems of Walt Whitman.

8. *Roy Harris* (1898–1979). His undisputed masterpiece is the Symphony No. 3, which could be said to have put American symphonic music on the map. Although the critic Deems Taylor said it sounded like people moving furniture around, it has weathered the test of time and emerged as one of the great symphonic statements of any era. His tremendous catalog includes fourteen symphonies and an outpouring of choral and chamber music. He taught at almost all of the great universities (Princeton, Cornell, UCLA, and many others) and was a significant influence on a generation of composers. Not bad for an Oklahoma boy who once worked as a milkman.

9. *Alan Hovhaness* (1911–2000). Every musical culture needs its mystics, its visionaries, and its ascetics, and he fit the bill in every respect. His enormous output may have reflected his concentration and single-mindedness. Best known for his symphony *Mysterious Mountain,* he achieved international fame, or at least notoriety, by composing an orchestral accompaniment to the recorded voices of sperm whales. His symphonies number well over sixty, and his executors are still compiling his unperformed and unpublished work.

10. *Charles Ives* (1874–1954). "Universally recognized as the first great American composer of concert music," says *Grove's Dictionary of American Music.* Leonard Bernstein called him "our musical Mark Twain, Emerson, and Lincoln all rolled into one." The titles of his best known works tell us all we need to know about his origins or his sympathies: *Three Places in New England, Decoration Day, The Fourth of July, The Concord Sonata,* and *Central Park in the Dark.* His Third Symphony, composed in 1904, had its first performance in 1946, and was promptly awarded the Pulitzer Prize. The rambunctious finale of his Second Symphony is fast becoming his—if not, indeed, America's—signature piece.

11. *Edward A. MacDowell* (1860–1908). Trained in Europe, he was better known there than in the United States, but when he returned to his homeland he quickly became the leading figure in American musical life. His two piano concertos are still in the repertory of leading pianists, and his piano pieces, among them "To a Wild Rose," are familiar to anyone who has ever studied that instrument. He may have been the first composer to have considered Native American traditions as a subject, and his *Indian Suite* is gaining new popularity as a result.

12. *Walter Piston* (1894–1976). His eight symphonies are as solid and enduring as his longtime associates, Harvard University and the Boston Symphony Orchestra. Another of the great teacher-composers, he taught at Harvard for over thirty years and wrote one of the great books on music theory, *Harmony,* published in 1941 and still in use in conservatories and universities throughout the world. His one theatrical work, the ballet *The Incredible Flutist,* is a favorite among orchestral musicians, who vie for the honor of barking like a dog during the crowd scene.

13. *John Philip Sousa* (1854–1932). The undisputed "March King," he is known throughout the world for his marches that seem to fit any occasion. In his own time he was better known for his leadership of the United States Marine Band, which he formed in 1892 and led until 1931. He also wrote much vocal music and operettas. This can be seen in his marches, such as *The Washington Post* and *The Stars and Stripes Forever,* which have a strong melodic line, as anyone who has ever attended summer camp knows. Who can ever forget "Be kind to your web-footed friends, for a duck may be somebody's mother"?

14. *William Grant Still* (1895–1978). The first African American composer to make his name in the concert music world. His *Afro-American Symphony* was premiered in 1930 by the Rochester Philharmonic Orchestra and was later featured by Leopold Stokowski leading the Philadelphia Orchestra, a heady beginning for any young composer. He went on to produce four more symphonies, ten operas, and numerous orchestral and instrumental pieces. His opera *A Bayou Legend* was produced on television in 1981. His later style became less folk and jazz oriented and, freed from its identification with a specific time and place, entered the mainstream of concert music. He eventually became known as a grand old man of American music.

**David Goodnough** is a freelance author who loves to listen to good music in Ossining, New York.

## Fourteen Great American Artists
BY ROBERTA SAVAGE

1. *Thomas Hart Benton* (1889–1975), an American regionalist painter, was born in Missouri. He was the son of a United States congressman and named after his granduncle, a Civil War senator. He is best known for his colorful murals of the 1930s, which depict American rural life. One of his finest murals is *America Today.* Other murals showing Missouri life are in the Truman Memorial Library in Independence. He was also an educator who taught at the Art Students League in New York City, where his most famous student was Jackson Pollock, and at the Kansas City Art Institute. He died in his studio in 1975.

2. *Thomas Cole* (1801–48), who is often credited with the founding of the American landscape school, was born in Lancashire, England. His family moved to the United States in 1818–19. He studied at the Pennsylvania Academy of the Fine Arts in Philadelphia beginning in 1823. In 1825 he moved to Catskill, New York, on the Hudson River, and was soon recognized as an important landscape painter. His fame attracted a group of painters who became known as the Hudson River School. His best known works include *The Oxbow* (1836) in the Metropolitan Museum of Art, New York City, and *The Course of Empire* (1836) in the New York Historical Society, New York City.

3. *Grant Wood* (1892–1942), a regionalist painter, with Benton and John Steuart Curry, and a teacher, is best known for his later paintings of scenes from his native Iowa. He studied at the Art Institute of Chicago and made several trips to Europe where he discovered sixteenth-century Flemish painting, a major influence on his work. His most famous painting, and an American icon, is the stylized realistic portrait *American Gothic. The Midnight Ride of Paul Revere* in the Metropolitan Museum of Art is an intriguing example of his landscape paintings. His irreverent treatment of the *Daughters of Revolution* reveals his wit and sense of irony.

4. *James Abbott McNeill Whistler* (1834–1903) achieved success as both a painter and an etcher and is considered one of the most important

nineteenth-century artists. He attended the United States Military Academy at West Point for several years but was dismisssed for failing in his studies. He moved to Paris in 1855 to pursue his long interest in drawing and art and never returned to the United States. He was acclaimed as an etcher in Paris but it was in London where he moved in about 1859 that his paintings found acceptance. His eccentric and flamboyant personality and his art led to international attention and interest. *Symphony in White No. 1: The White Girl* was a great attraction at the Paris Salon des Refusés after being rejected from the official Salon. His abstract landscapes titled *Nocturnes* were shocking to the English public. His best known portrait is *Arrangement in Black and Grey No. 1: The Artist's Mother,* also known as *Whistler's Mother.*

5. *Robert Burns Motherwell* (1915–91) was one of the founders of abstract expressionism and one of its most widely recognized and prolific practitioners. Unusual among American abstract expressionists, he was an abstract painter from the beginning. His first solo exhibition was in New York City in 1944. A series of often large paintings titled *Elegy to the Spanish Republic* was inspired by the Spanish Civil War and has become one of his best known works. The series contains more than one hundred images mostly painted in black on a white ground. He has had one-man exhibitions worldwide.

6. *Mary Cassatt* (1844–1926), who was born in Pennsylvania and began to study painting at the Pennsylvania Academy of the Fine Arts in Philadelphia, is best known as an impressionist painter who lived and worked in France. Though she was an expatriate she considered herself an American, and two paintings she sent to the Society of American Artists, established in 1877, were some of the first impressionist paintings seen in America. She was influenced, as were many of the Impressionists, by Japanese art and woodcuts. A theme throughout many of her paintings is the close relationship between mothers and children. Some of her best known paintings include *The Boating Party, The Cup of Tea,* and *The Mirror.*

7. *Andy Warhol* (1928–1987) was a painter, printmaker, and movie director who was a major artist of the pop art movement and twentieth-century American popular culture. He was born Andrew Warhola in Pittsburgh,

Pennsylvania, and studied at the Carnegie Institute of Technology. After working successfully as a commercial artist, he began exhibiting paintings and silkscreens in New York City. The subjects were objects from everyday life, such as *Campbell's Soup Can,* and popular culture icons such as *Marilyn Monroe.* His experimental movies include *Empire,* a seven-hour film of the Empire State Building, *The Chelsea Girls,* and *Trash.*

8. *Alexander Calder* (1898–1976) was an American sculptor best known for his innovative mobile and stabile sculptures. Born in Lawton, Pennsylvania, the son of two generations of sculptors, he developed sculpture in motion. His often-monumental mobiles and stabiles are some of the most popular abstract works and can be found in public spaces in American cities and worldwide. A small-scale circus, sculpted in wire with other materials, which he used in performances and is often displayed at the Whitney Museum of American Art in New York City, shows his wit and humor. He has been exhibited and honored worldwide.

9. *Georgia O'Keeffe* (1887–1986) was an American abstract painter whose still lifes and landscapes are both sensual and austere. She was born in Wisconsin and studied at the Art Institute of Chicago and the Art Students League. Her work was exhibited at 291, Alfred Stieglitz's gallery in New York City. She married Alfred Stieglitz, the photographer and gallery director, in 1924. She inspired him to produce more than five hundred photographs of her, a many-faceted portrait. Much of her life was lived in New Mexico, and her paintings of the desert and bleached bones are some of her most recognized. Her close-up paintings of flowers, such as *Black Iris,* are sensuous and visionary. Entranced by views from an airplane, she painted *Sky Above Clouds,* a twenty-four-foot-wide mural.

10. *Edward Hopper* (1882–1967) was an individualist painter of an American realism characterized by a sense of solitude, loneliness, and alienation. His paintings, mostly of New York or New England, show people in shadowed night scenes, landscapes of remote lighthouses, empty city streets with old buildings or darkened, moody interiors. Light and mood are the real subjects of his paintings. One of his best known works is *Nighthawks,* showing isolated customers in an all-night café.

11. *Jackson Pollock* (1912–56), a (possibly the) leading painter of the abstract expressionist movement, developed a distinctive style of action painting that abandoned the traditional ideas of composition. Even his early work, as a student of Thomas Hart Benton, shows this all-over rhythmic brush stroke, which in his later work he accomplished by dripping and pouring the paint from a can or stick onto the canvas, which was tacked to the floor. *Full Fathom Five,* a painting done by this method, achieved an overall web created of paint and objects such as nails, cigarette butts, and tacks stuck in the paint. He had many one-man shows and became one of the most influential artists in America. He died in an automobile accident in 1956.

12. *Jacob Lawrence* (1917–2000) was born in Atlantic City, New Jersey, and moved with his mother to Harlem in 1930 where he studied with Charles Alston at the Harlem Community Art Center. He became an educator as well as a painter and taught at Pratt Institute in Brooklyn, New York, and the University of Washington in Seattle. He is best known for his paintings of narrative scenes based on African American history and figures. Two of his more famous works are *The Harriett Tubman Series* (thirty panels) and *The Migration Series* (sixty paintings). His strong, vivid, graphic images show the influence of expressionism and cubism.

13. *Winslow Homer* (1836–1910), a much-admired painter and graphic artist, is considered one of the greatest nineteenth-century American naturalistic painters. Born in Boston, Massachusetts, he was basically a self-taught artist who had little formal training. His work as a watercolorist was as important to him as his oil paintings. Many of his paintings had the sea as their subject; other subjects included children and rural farm life. Some of his most famous paintings are *Snap the Whip, The Northeaster,* and the watercolor *Hurricane, Bahamas.*

14. *Thomas Eakins* (1844–1916) was the foremost American realist painter of the nineteenth century. He was born in Philadelphia and studied at the Pennsylvania Academy of the Fine Arts. Studying anatomy at Jefferson Medical College in Philadelphia and academic art training at the École des Beaux-Arts in Paris were also part of his education. People and scenes around him in Philadelphia were his main subjects. Many of his models were family and

friends. His early masterpiece was *The Gross Clinic,* a hospital scene of an operation. Some other fine works include *Max Schmitt in a Single Scull* and the portrait of Mrs. Letitia Bacon.

**Roberta Savage** of Ossining, New York, is art director for Maryknoll, the Catholic Foreign Mission Society of America. A graduate from Pratt Institute, one of her teachers was Jacob Lawrence.

As Americans of various races, we share a broad cultural background, a commonality of society that links its diverse elements into a cohesive whole that can be defined as "American."

—August Wilson, American playwright

Although the original ideals handed down to us by our Founders were almost perfect expressions of a commitment to human justice, America has never fully manifested those ideals. That does not mean that we are bad or hypocritical, but merely a nation still in the throes of a greater becoming. We have, from our beginning, been home to both noble and spiritually based political impulses, as well as to the most materialistic and selfish ones. Freedom means that we will be as a nation whatever we, the people, choose to be. The push and pull between two major aspects of our being is the overarching drama of our national life.

—Marianne Williamson, American author
*The Healing of America*

Chapter Eleven

# THE AMERICAN CHALLENGE

Posterity—you will never know how much it has cost my generation to preserve your freedom. I hope you will make good use of it.

> —John Quincy Adams
> Sixth President of the United States

Our country, right or wrong. When right to be kept right, when wrong to be put right.

> —Carl Schurz, American statesman,
> in speech to Congress, 1872

I believe in the goodness of a free society. And I believe the society can remain good only as long as we are willing to fight for it—and to fight against whatever imperfections may exist.

> —Jackie Robinson, American athlete

We are learning in this crisis not just to save ourselves but to save each other.

> —Julia Roberts, American actress

The future which we hold in trust for our own children will be shaped by our fairness to other people's children.

> —Marian Wright Edelman
> American humanitarian

Mercy Corps's Dan O'Neill in Kosovo in 1996 with a three-year-old Albanian: "Our moral compass . . ."

## The Compassionate Touch

BY DAN O'NEILL

My national birthright has blessed me with bounty beyond measure: a land of breathtaking physical beauty, economic opportunity, impressive technology, rich demographic diversity, unparalleled freedoms, and civil rights underpinned by the rule of law. The sweeping possibilities for American citizens are without equal anywhere.

A perfect country? No. A dynamic destination sought by multitudes from every quarter of our planet? Yes. There are no rivers of American refugees streaming out of our nation. Millions are praying to get in.

Though we Americans have been battered and stained and rightly blamed by many who have been hurt by less than enlightened foreign policies over the years, we remain a beacon of hope, an umbrella of shelter, and a source of goodwill to a very large degree. And we continue to learn how to be an even better global neighbor by lessons learned in both victories and defeats.

As we take the measure of our national moral character, we must always hearken to the cries of the least of these—those in our world who are hungry, homeless, powerless, voiceless, poor, sick, oppressed, and otherwise marginalized. Our moral compass will be continuously recalibrated as we contemplate our responses to emerging human crises and tragedies. God knows there are, sadly, endless painful flashpoints of urgent need to keep us honing our "True North" navigational skills for many decades to come. We must see these as opportunities to show courage and authentic compassion.

The American challenge is the challenge to be our best selves.

I have been blessed to witness a refreshingly generous spirit by millions of Americans who support humanitarian organizations like Mercy Corps, an energetic, innovative agency touching the lives of 5 million hurting people in twenty-five countries annually through emergency relief services, long-term development programs, and civil society strategies in some of the most explosive hot spots imaginable. Caring American donor partners enthusiastically sponsor outreach projects bringing real help to real people every minute of every day.

It may be fitting an Afghan refugee child with an artificial limb to restore a mine-shattered leg. It may be feeding a starving little girl in the bleakest famine-stricken village of North Korea. Or helping Serb and Albanian families find collaborative business ventures to help create conditions for peace in the aftermath of destructive interethnic, interreligious conflict in Kosovo.

These scenarios restore my faith in our citizens who, when linked to organizations like ours, are actually making the world a better place for all of God's children.

Yes, we are a fabulously wealthy country, the only real superpower. And, yes, to whom much is given, much is required. Power, money, and technology can all be used for destructive, manipulative purposes. We must use them as precious assets for constructive, humane endeavors. If we follow that moral compass, there is no end to the good we can achieve together. There is no doubt that we still struggle with what this means collectively and individually. But growing we most certainly are, as we heal from our wounds and press ahead to embrace a vision of peace and justice for all.

We will do the things that matter most. We will share the compassionate touch.

We will be Americans.

**Dan O'Neill** is president and cofounder of Mercy Corps, a not-for-profit organization headquartered in Portland, Oregon, that exists to alleviate suffering, poverty, and oppression throughout the world by helping people build secure, productive, and just communities.

What does it mean to be an American? For most young Americans I know, "serving" in a broad sense seems like the only thing to do.
—Chelsea Clinton, university student
*Seventeen*

Never doubt that a small group of thoughtful, committed citizens can change the world; indeed, it is the only thing that ever has.

—Margaret Mead, American
anthropologist

What does it mean to be American? To have pride in our country, but also to realize we're not alone in the world.

—Katie Harman, Miss America 2002
*Seventeen*

[After working with his wife in an Ethiopian orphanage for six weeks]—You'd wake up in the morning, and mist would be lifting. You'd walk out of your tent and you'd count bodies of dead and abandoned children. Or worse, the father of a child would walk up to you and try to give you his living child and say, "You take it, because if this is your child, it won't die. . . ." There is no justification for denying the very poorest countries market access. . . . *(Let us accompany the war against terrorism)* with the pursuit of a less dangerous world . . . one where "America" is once again a great idea, contagious and inclusive.

—Bono, Irish rock star, *Time*

To be true to ourselves, we must be true to others. We will not behave in foreign places so as to violate our rules and standards here at home, for we know that the trust which our nation earns is essential to our strength.

The world itself is now dominated by a new spirit. Peoples more numerous and more politically aware are craving and now demanding their place in the sun—not just for the benefit of their own physical condition, but for basic human rights.

The passion for freedom is on the rise. Tapping this new spirit, there can be no nobler nor more ambitious task for America to undertake on this day of a new beginning than to help shape a just and peaceful world that is truly humane.

—Jimmy Carter
Thirty-ninth President of the
United States

The history of America is now the central feature of the history of the world; for the world has set its face hopefully toward our democracy; and, O my fellow citizens, each one of you carries on your shoulders not only the burden of doing well for the sake of your own country, but the burden of doing well and of seeing that this nation does well for the sake of mankind.

—Theodore Roosevelt
Twenty-sixth President of the
United States

America is the globe's leading nation, but for all our power, we can rarely succeed simply by going it alone. And if we want the world to take our views into account, we must at least listen to the concerns of others. We must listen to allies who ask us to join in banning nuclear explosive tests and who want us to preserve space as a laboratory for science, not an arena for a new kind of war. We must listen to scientists who say global warming is real and a threat to our future, and who believe that conservation is the key to a sound energy policy, not a four-letter word. We must listen to those whose voices are sometimes the hardest to hear: to the millions afflicted with HIV-AIDS; and those caught up in the conflict in Chechnya and Sudan; for those praying to an end to violence in the Middle East; and the women and minorities of Afghanistan.

—Madeleine Albright, in an address to
the Brown University Class of 2001,
May 27, 2001

*The Corporal Works of Mercy*

1. Feed the hungry
2. Give drink to the thirsty
3. Clothe the naked
4. Visit the imprisoned
5. Shelter the homeless
6. Visit the sick
7. Bury the dead

We were just sitting there talking when Peter Maurin came in.

We were just sitting there talking when lines of people began to form, saying, "We need bread." We could not say, "Go, be thou filled." If there were six small loaves and a few fishes, we had to divide them. There was always bread.

We were just sitting there talking and people moved in on us. Let those who can take it, take it. Some moved out and that made room for more. And somehow the walls expanded.

We were just sitting there talking and someone said, "Let's all go and live on a farm."

It was as casual as all that, I often think. It just came about. It just happened.

I found myself, a barren woman, the joyful mother of children. It is not easy always to be joyful, to keep in mind the duty of delight.

The most significant thing about the Catholic Worker is poverty, some say.

The most significant thing is community, others say. We are not alone anymore.

But the final word is love. At times it has been, in the words of Father Zossima, a harsh and dreadful thing, and our very faith in love has been tried through fire.

We cannot love God unless we love each other. We know Him in the breaking of bread, and we know each other in the breaking of bread, and we are not alone anymore. Heaven is a banquet and life is a banquet, too, even with a crust, where there is companionship.

We have all known the long loneliness and we have learned that the only solution is love and that love comes with community.

It all happened while we sat there talking, and it is still going on.

—Dorothy Day, American peace and
justice activist, *The Long Loneliness*


Teach your children what we have taught our children, that the earth is our mother. Whatever befalls the earth befalls the children of the earth. If we spit upon the ground, we spit upon ourselves. This we know. The earth does not belong to us; we belong to the earth.

One thing we know, which the white man may one day discover, our God is the same God. You may think now that you own

Him as you wish to own the land; but you cannot. He is the God of all people and His compassion is equal for all. The earth is precious to God, and to harm the earth is to heap contempt on its creator.

So love it as we have loved it. Care for it as we have cared for it. And with all your mind, with all your heart, preserve it for your children and love as God loves all.

—Chief Seattle, 1851

I hate war as only a soldier who has lived it can, only as one who has seen its brutality, its futility, its *stupidity.*

> —Dwight D. Eisenhower
> Thirty-fourth President of the
> United States

War is an invention of the human mind. The human mind can invent peace.

> —Norman Cousins, American editor
> *Who Speaks for Man?*

"We the people of the United States" now form the most profusely religious nation on earth. But many, if not most, Christian, Jewish, or secular Americans have never visited a mosque or a Hindu or Buddhist temple. Many Americans are not so sure what Sikhs or Muslims believe, let alone Jains and Zoroastrians. Similarly, Muslim or Hindu Americans may have sketchy and stereotypical views of Christians and Jews. So where do we go from here? It's one thing to be unconcerned about or ignorant of Muslim or Buddhist neighbors on the other side of the world, but when Buddhists are our next-door neighbors, when our children are best friends with Muslim classmates, when a Hindu is running for a seat on the school committee, all of us have a new vested interest in our neighbors, both as citizens and as people of faith.

As the new century dawns, we Americans are challenged to make good on the promise of religious freedom so basic to the very idea and image of America. Religious freedom has always given rise to religious diversity, and never has our diversity been more dramatic than it is today. This will require us to reclaim the deepest meaning of the very principles we cherish and to create a truly pluralistic American society in which this great diversity is not simply tolerated but becomes the very source of our strength. But to do this, we will all need to know more than we do about one another and to listen for the new ways in which new Americans articulate the "we" and contribute to the sound and spirit of America.

—Diana L. Eck, American educator
*A New Religious America*

All of my life I've felt privileged to have had good friends around me, privileged to have been able to do the kind of work I know and love the best, and to have been born in a country whose immense beauty and grandeur are matched only by the greatness of her people. . . .

I know most of you feel the same as I do about some of her imperfections, but sometimes that's good. Especially if it gets us working together to make things better. It seems to me we often take too much for granted, and have a tendency to forget "the Good Things about America."

My hope and prayer is that everyone know and love our country for what she really is and what she stands for. May we nurture her strengths and strengthen her weaknesses so that she will always be a "Land of the Free, and Home of the Brave."

—John Wayne, American actor
*America, Why I Love Her*

## The Soul of America
### BY JACOB NEEDLEMAN

Herein lies the secret of America—that it still has the future, that it offers mankind a future. The remnants of other nations and cultures may strike the sense of wonder in us with the greatness of their art and beauty and customs. But in these places we are looking into the past. In America, we are looking into the future—maybe an increasingly threatening future, but still a real one. America's spaces still exist, its vast stretches of nature—mountains, deserts, forests. America is still raw, still unplumbed, undeveloped. Spatially and temporally, America is still unfinished—as man, the unfinished animal, is still and ever not yet what he can become.

It is what man is now and what he can become that is the real, inner meaning of time and the future as the prophet understands these words. If we take America "literally," if we see around us conformity and vulgarity, metaphysical squalor and blind attachment to physical comfort—if we see only that, we see the death of America and the end of its future. But if we look more deeply, we may still see a nation and a people granted for a brief moment the material and spiritual conditions enabling them to step into the real future of man, that is the future of the developing soul.

*The future is another word for the soul.* And the only hope for man is in the growth of the soul: such, uncompromisingly and without any possibility of bargaining, is the message of the teachings of wisdom, those very teachings whose reflection, however faint, gave original light to the ideals of the American nation.

We still have the future. America has the future in its grasp, though that grasp is weakening. Other nations and peoples have the past—and, flowing through the past to this continent, our continent, a new world was born: in pain, in sorrow, in greed, in corruption, in injustice, in the enslavement and murder of the masses—but it was born; and nowhere on earth have worlds been born independently of the crimes of man—except for the inner worlds, the second history of the earth that flows within and amid the violent, confused first history of the earth. America was born and with it, the flame of the future—the flame of hope—was transmitted.

Our first and last question is this: Can America, with its great armies protecting itself and the world, with its Constitution lighting the way to empowering the peoples of the world—can America become both stronger and weaker than it now is? Weaker in the sense of allowing itself and the world to remember what it stands for—namely, the vision that requires of the individual a higher, invisible reality; stronger in that it begins to remember what it was created to protect and shelter: the process by which men and women seek to tend the soul.

Can America remember that it exists in the world and—in some way we do not understand—may even have been *allowed* to become so strong, in order to protect that upon which all the great civilizations of history have been based? America means the melting pot, yes, but not only of races and people but of the wisdom by which all races and peoples have sought to live. As the instrument of the unstoppable processes of modernity which are destroying the forms of traditional cultures, can America realize that it must assume the great task of helping to bring to the earth that which the great civilizations of the world once brought to the earth: namely, the teachings of wisdom and the path that wisdom offers its children, which leads to the soul's birth within the earth body.

**Jacob Needleman,** professor of philosophy at San Francisco State University, is the author of many books, including *The American Soul.*

We have a place, all of us, in a long story, a story we continue, but whose end we will not see. It is the American story, a story of flawed and fallible people, united across the generations by grand and enduring ideals. The grandest of these ideals is an unfolding American promise: that everyone belongs, that everyone deserves a chance, that no insignificant person was ever born. Americans are called to enact this promise in our lives and in our laws. And though our nation has sometimes halted, and sometimes delayed, we must follow no other course.

—George W. Bush
Forty-third President of the
United States

And so, my fellow Americans: ask not what your country can do for you—ask what you can do for your country. My fellow citizens of the world: ask not what America will do for you, but what together we can do for the freedom of man.

—John F. Kennedy
Thirty-fifth President of the
United States

Alone we can do little.
Together we can do so much.

—Helen Keller, American inspiration

# EPILOGUE

The more American America can be, the better it will be for America. Let us not copy other countries. Let us not copy Europe, because it is our destiny to be America. Do not copy England; God has done England once, and done it very well, but he does not want to do it again here, because God does not repeat Himself. Let us not copy France; God has done France once, and done it very well, and He does not want to repeat that either. Let us not copy Germany, or Italy, or any other country in the world; but be ourselves. If we must make mistakes, in Heaven's name, let us make our own mistakes and not somebody else's. When we do make our own mistakes, we learn a tremendous lot, and, if we suffer too, it is worthwhile, because we learn. But when we make somebody else's mistakes, we suffer just the same, and we learn nothing at all. The more American America can be, the faster she will advance; the better off her people will be; and the more she will help the whole world.

Remember that America is not to be just a new copy of something old, but something quite new, and, therefore, something better than anything that has gone before.

—Emmet Fox, American teacher
*Alter Your Life*

# ACKNOWLEDGMENTS

I am grateful to the many contributors whose original stories illumine this book, and to the publishers who gave permission to reprint sparkling excerpts from their books, magazines, and newspapers.

I am particularly grateful to my colleague Therese Borchard who encouraged me to do this book and lent a hand along the way (look for Therese's new book, *I Like Being a Mom,* which comes to a bookstore near you in 2004 and will be in print forever after). Thanks, too, to other good friends from sea to shining sea who pitched in with ideas and suggestions, especially the ever-encouraging Bob Elliott, and also Ned Scharff, Dom and Bonnie Butera, Tom Bruce, Greg Pierce, Bill Burke, Wendy Wright, Doris Goodnough, Robert Ellsberg, Tim Unsworth, Steven Harrison, Arthur Vegara, and anyone I failed to mention (please forgive me).

A special thanks goes to my agent, Joe Durepos, for his enthusiasm and to all the professionals at Doubleday who helped turn the words and ideas in *I Like Being American* into the beautiful book you hold in your hands, particularly Eric Major, Elizabeth Walter, and Michelle Rapkin.

Most of all, love and gratitude to Vickie, spouse and best friend, for her love and gratitude every day of our life.

# CREDITS

The editor has endeavored to credit all known persons holding copyright or reproduction rights for passages quoted and for illustrations reproduced in this book, especially:

American Federation of Teachers, for excerpt from "Where We Stand," November 2001, monthly column by Sandra Feldman.

American Immigration Law Foundation, for "Why I Am Glad America Is a Nation of Immigrants" by Crystal Uvalle.

Amy-Beth Pitura, for group photographs.

Anne Kertz-Kernion (www.cardssbyanne.com) for artwork/calligraphy on frontispiece.

Ballantine Books, as secondary source for some scripture quotes found in *Oneness: Great Principles Shared by All Religions* by Jeffrey Moses. Used with permission.

Bantam Books, a division of Random House, Inc., for excerpt from *Iacocca: An Autobiography* by Lee Iacocca. Copyright © 1984 by Lee Iacocca. Used by permission.

Batjack Productions, for excerpt from *America, Why I Love Her* by John Wayne.

Bettman/CORBIS, for photographs of Cary Grant, Audrey Hepburn, Greta Garbo, and Albert Einstein.

Builders of the Adytum, Ltd., for excerpt from *The Great Seal of the United States* by Paul Foster Case.

Chicago Cubs, for photograph of Sammy Sosa.

of America," December 3, 2001. Copyright © 2001 by Anna Quindlen. Reprinted with permission.

Iranian.com and Setareh Sabety for "No Walls" by Setareh Sabety.

The Jacques Maritain Center, University of Notre Dame, for excerpt from *Reflections on America* by Jacques Maritain.

Jeremy P. Tarcher, a division of Penguin Putnam, Inc., for excerpt from *The American Soul* by Jacob Needleman. Copyright © 2002 by Jacob Needleman.

Louis Glanzman, for painting *July 5th 1776.*

Mitchell Gerber/CORBIS, for photograph of Iman.

Missionary Sisters of the Sacred Heart of Jesus, Stella Maris Province, for photograph of Mother Cabrini.

National Public Radio, *All Things Considered,* and Dinesh D'Souza for "The Idea of America" by Dinesh D'Souza.

Newsweek, Inc., for excerpt from "An Immigrant's Faith" by Fareed Zakaria from *Newsweek,* December 24, 2001. All rights reserved.

Niko Plaitakis, for photograph *Love* near the site of Ground Zero.

Parade Publications, for excerpt by Alex Haley, first published in *Let Freedom Ring,* Continuum, New York, 1992. Reprinted with permission. Copyright © 2002.

Parade Publications, for excerpt by Joyce Brothers first published in *Let Freedom Ring,* Continuum, New York, 1992. Reprinted with permission. Copyright © 2002.

Parade Publications, January 14, 2001, and Bill O'Reilly for excerpt from *What's Right With America* by Bill O'Reilly. Reprinted with permission. Copyright © 2001.

Parade Publications, July 10, 1994, and Daniel Boorstin for excerpt from *I Am Optimistic About America* by Daniel Boorstin. Reprinted with permission. Copyright © 1994.

Salon.com, August 1997, for excerpt from essay by Chitra Divakaruni.